A Pixie's Prescription

A Fun Toolkit for A Feel Better Life

BY KATE CHAPMAN

The content of this book is for general instruction only. Each person's physical, emotional, and spiritual condition is unique. The instruction in this book is not intended to replace or interrupt the reader's relationship with a physician or other professional. Please consult your doctor for matters pertaining to your specific health and diet.

For My Mom
– who always worked hard to make sure I was "well".

And for My Husband, Ed
– who loved me even though I was so very sick.

Introduction:
A Pixie's Prescription

For years I was like so many Americans still are today. I was physically encumbered by excess weight. I desperately wanted to lose the weight and regain my formerly thin self before it was "too late". At the age of 34 I embarked on a journey that has led me here: To a place of wellness, health, and a consistently thin self. I only set out to lose weight, but I gained a full, healthy life as a beautiful side effect.

For the first time in my dieting history, I didn't strive to count calories, measure portions, and have my life revolve around edible substances. Instead, I chose to educate myself about what foods make my body well, and what foods make my body sick. Throughout my exploration I found that the only absolute when it comes to the human body is that it likes to eat vegetables, and that those vegetables can help a body heal itself in remarkable ways.

Through my time losing one hundred pounds I learned a lot about physical foods. I also learned that most of my problems with weight had very little to do with what I ate, and much more with what I fed my overall self. I reconnected with the ideas of play, curiosity, creativity, relationships, social interaction, education, spirituality, home cooking, exercise, finances, joy, career, health, and my home environment. I noticed how those aspects of my life were important components in my personal well-being. I also noticed that if I wasn't feeding them, I wasn't well.

After a few years of regarding "My Sparkly Daisy" – with petals named after each of the attributes of life I needed to attend to, and surrounding a center of play and a supporting stem of curiosity – I encountered Joshua Rosenthal and his school The Institute for Integrative Nutrition. Joshua teaches a concept called Primary Foods – which are all the aspects of my daisy, minus the center and stem. I was elated to find someone else who regarded these "foods" as necessary for personal health and wellbeing.

Once I finished my studies at IIN (to become a Health Coach) and started my practice, I realized my clients were hungrier for Primary Foods than the ones they were physically chewing. I felt I wanted to add to the conversation started by Joshua, and add my Sparkly Daisy to the mix. When I center my life around play and support it with curiosity, I find I remain healthy, happy, well, and excited to greet each and every new day.

I started this journey hoping to lose weight. I did that. I lost one hundred pounds, and have consistently maintained that weight loss for over six years. But I also lost all the other diseases I had carried with me for years. I got busy living my life to the fullest, growing my flower, and adding beauty to my world...and all the sickness shriveled up and died away in the process. I'm not a doctor – but I've been treated by a lot of them. I've even been treated by some of the best in the world. What I know is that they didn't cure me. Implementing my Free Fairy Food did. I'm not telling anyone to stop seeing medical doctors. I'm simply adding a fun, free, effective prescription to the pile. I hope those of you who are searching for another way might try it for yourself. A Pixie's Prescription is truly affordable health care. And it's fun, too.

Pixie's Rx – Overall Health

This Book – Use this book like an old-style physician's bag of medicine. Reach in, find what you're looking for, and quickly administer the cure. The stories are here just to highlight a petal of my daisy and to add some insight into another person's journey. The Yumspirations don't have measurements – as I don't cook that way. Use your tastes as your guide. Smell the ingredient. How much of that do you want in your food? Put that much in. It's simply about personal taste. And, keep in mind, as with any journey into messing around inside your Body, Mind, or Spirit – do so with respect, reverence, and attention to how you're doing in the process. There is no rush to find that which feeds you and makes you nourished and whole. And, as in all things in life, it will constantly be changing. Enjoy the exploration each day. Utilize as many tools as you can, when you can, and know that health is not a science or a religion. It's a journey. There is no one right path. Get help where and when you need to. And to help you out right now, here are some "freeways" to travel.... Enjoy the journey!

Table of Contents
The Parts of the Daisy

Chapter 1
-Curiosity-

The How of Now

"How" is my favorite question word. "How" implies an answer that is a solution. "How" shows me what to do, in what order, and when. "How" makes me happy. I think it's because "how" ignites my Curiosity. And when I'm Curious, I feel alive, invested in the world around me, and hopeful of connecting with others who might be able to answer my questions.

I remember hearing the old adage "Curiosity killed the cat" as a little girl. Often I was counselled NOT to be Curious. As an adult I wholeheartedly disagree. Curiosity doesn't have to be dangerous. It can be safe and now there are people studying longevity and the correlation that Curiosity has to it. Turns out that Curious people might live LONGER than those who aren't. Whether or not the studies go on to "prove" anything or not is beside the point for me. I know that when I am Curious, I connect to life. And when I connect to life, I'm my very best self.

These days I'm mainly Curious about other peoples' stories – and mushrooms. I vacillate between the two. What I'd really love is to be able to hear the mushrooms' stories and then to be able to experience *being* one! And then write – and star in – a musical about the secret lives of mushrooms. But since that isn't a viable option, I imagine mushrooms' lives and listen to the stories I *can* hear from humans.

I love to hear stories from people who live a totally different life from mine. I love stories from decades before I was born. I really love stories from distant lands, places I can only imagine. And then I like to share those stories with others in order to pique their Curiosity. Someone else's story

1

combined with my experience of hearing it becomes a whole other tale in and of itself.

Some of my favorite stories to tell are from my time in Uganda. Usually, before I can even get a tale going, the word "Uganda" sparks the question, "Why did you go *there*?" I have two quick answers for that: 1. I was Curious; and 2. I was asked. It's that simple. Mostly, I was Curious. What was Africa like? What would it feel like to be a minority? How would I deal with living so far outside of my norm? I had thousands of questions for myself. So, when I was offered the opportunity, I simply said "yes".

In Uganda I got to hear a lot of people's stories. I found the tales to be incredibly diverse and yet they could have basically been told by any one of us, just changing a few things here and there. I love to hear what people choose to share with me. I love to sense when something is being withheld or edited. And I LOVE to hear a tale told by a person used to commanding attention.

On my last day in Uganda I met such a storyteller. This man was staying in our hotel complex and when I saw him across the garden from his "hut", I knew who he was immediately. My gut fluttered with excitement the moment I saw him, and when he motioned me over to him I was thrilled. I had wanted to meet him from the first moment I knew he was staying in "Disneyland Uganda", as I called our hotel.

Disneyland Uganda was an oasis in the middle of an otherwise unpleasant city. Kampala is not well appointed, well designed, nor well cared for. But inside the electrified gates of Disneyland Uganda, life is beautiful. Nicely dressed Ugandans take care of your every want and need. The rooms are made to look like thatched roof huts and are surrounded by gloriously cared for gardens.

The establishment is owned by a couple from India who, while lovely, have a skewed view of the country in which they are now making their home. They don't even see how condescending the design of their property is to the very people hired to care for it. However, as an American used to a certain standard of living, I was hypocritically grateful when the guards shut the gate behind our borrowed car each evening. I knew their AK47s would be used for my protection, should that be necessary, and I found comfort in that fact.

In actuality that wasn't quite true. The guards with AK47s were there to protect my new friend in the garden, not me. I knew this because our Ambassador host had told us days earlier we were now staying "with the Congolese Rebels". The minute I heard those words, I was Curious. What does a Congolese Rebel look like? Would I know one when I saw him? Would they be wearing tribal wear or have some sort of body manipulation art like the neck stretchers? How would I feel when I met one?

By the last morning of my stay, however, I hadn't seen anyone who would have been, in my uneducated opinion, a rebel from the Congo. I had seen plenty of Dutch filmmakers, but no rebels. I had actually given up the search a few days prior – disappointed not to have seen them. However, since so many other incredible things HAD happened, on the last morning I was slowly walking around the garden assimilating them into clear thoughts when I saw him – looking nothing at all like "a rebel". In fact, other than being about seven feet tall, he looked "normal". But I knew instantly who he was.

On my second pass by his hut, I was summoned over. With what seemed like a magnetic pull, I walked slowly to him. As I arrived he said, "You're here cleansing your aura and aligning your chakras, aren't you?" I gave an embarrassed giggle. "Yes, I guess that's what I am here doing." Then he gazed in to my eyes, extended his right hand and said, "Hello. I am Lawrence, from the Congo." I'm sure my eyes flashed with excitement as I offered, "Hi, I'm Kate, from New York City."

3

As soon as I said that, he grasped my right hand within both of his giant hands and said, "You're the Broadway actress who sang here the other night, correct? I'm so sorry I was unable to attend. I heard you are very good." I'm sure I blushed. He went on to say he knew I was part of the new musical being done in Kampala, and that he was happy to meet me. I asked him what he was doing in Kampala – even though I knew: He was in peace negotiations with the government of the Congo, representing the faction M23.

Lawrence didn't share any of that with me. Instead he said, "I am here (long pause) – on Business." "Oh," I smirked, "is your business going well?" He answered a cryptic, "We shall see." And then we began sharing stories, ideas, thoughts about the world, religion, autism, health, The Arts, and a host of offshoot subjects. His manner was gentle, easy, relaxed, warm, and he felt, in a way, enlightened to me.

After an hour of standing in the middle of Fake Africa inside our Disneyland-like hotel discussing very real things, we said our goodbyes. He invited me to say hello to him if I saw him again, even if he was in a meeting. That blew my mind! The Rebel With A Cause felt I was engaging enough to merit an interruption in solving international conflict. I silently vowed to keep my eyes open for him throughout that final day before my 2 a.m. flight to Istanbul. I wanted to feel the energy put forth by those he was negotiating with.

As he grabbed my attention back from my Curiosity flight of fancy of meeting "the other side", he said, "I believe women are the saviors of this world. Men destroy. Women create life and are nurturers of it. Please keep doing the work you're doing, Kate Chapman, and encourage your fellow sisters to rise up as well. And can I ask you one favor?" I, of course, said an emphatic, "Yes!" He began, "Each night as you lay down to sleep, close your eyes, replay your day in reverse, and ask yourself, 'How much was I asleep during my day?' Each day, try to wake up a little more and for a little longer. Don't waste your life by sleeping through it. Be

4

awake." And then I felt he implied, "And eat all your vegetables!"

Pixie's Rx

Just A Quick Question – Make a list of questions you've always wondered about, like "Why do mosquitoes buzz so close to your ears?" or "How does chocolate make me so happy?" Just list a bunch of questions. Then, seek out "answers". I don't mean definitive truths – just explanations. Make up your own answers. Research. Ask others. Give yourself the benefit of a quick question – and answer – per day. Why not?

What's Under This Rock? – Go outside. Find a good-sized rock that prohibits grass-growth below and turn it over. Do you see the whole universe of creatures crawling under there? Good. Spend some time looking at their world. Who tries to escape when the rock goes away? Who plays dead? What shapes are the tunnels in the soil? How does this remind me of my world? Be Curious about stuff that lies beneath the surface that is usually really cool.

Replay My Day – I love that I have a "before sleep task" inside my head. I have taken Lawrence's charge one-step further. After I've replayed my day and assessed how much I was awake in it, I ask myself three questions: 1. How did I feel about who I was today? 2. How many times was I playing someone else? 3. How do I want to be tomorrow? As I drift off to sleep, I feel calm yet excited for the coming day. Not all days are fun to replay, but when I do it anyway I am always glad I did. Ending with my 3 questions moves me out of one place and into another, better place.

Tell Me More About That – When I trained as a Health Coach at The Institute for Integrative Nutrition, I learned the value of this sentence. The founder and main teacher, Joshua Rosenthal, very often comes back to this sentence as a means of helping a client delve deeper into their story. As I got used to saying this to my clients, however, I noticed how little I would say it to the people closest to me. Nobody I was closest to was getting as much Curiosity from me as they deserved, so I decided to employ this with the people I love, too. My husband can now tell me much more . . . simply because I say, 'Tell me more about that.'

If It's Broken . . . Look Inside – I remember watching TV as a child and seeing some kid on the screen taking apart a radio. I loved how it looked all in pieces, but I also knew I wasn't someone who would be able to put it back together well, so I never took a screwdriver to anything that was initially whole. However, when things break – and it's not economical to have them fixed – I take them apart and have a look inside. I love seeing and touching all the different parts of things. And, I usually come away with a better understanding of how something works! One of these days I'm going to start fixing stuff, too!

Be Like Gladys Kravitz – While I'm not advising becoming a nosy neighbor, as such, what she really was, in effect, was a Curious woman. Why were there strange things going on at the Stevens' house? How did Samantha make people appear and disappear? Find something that baffles you – like, poor Gladys was baffled by Samantha on "Bewitched" – and keep seeking out answers to your questions. But don't make your neighbors mad!

Seek Out A Master Craftsman – I love when I meet A Master – someone who has practiced something so much (over 10,000 hours) that they can amaze me with their proficiency. When I see my girl Mary Ann play the piano, I'm entranced. How does she get such a huge sound out of a piano? When I see my friend Tachi's decorating work I wonder how he makes everything SO perfect. So I ask. How do they begin? What is their process? And when I meet strangers who are Masters, I ask them questions, too. If I don't ask, I can never become A Master too . . . and I love to be masterful! Ask me how!

Take A Different Route – I find I get caught in taking the same path again and again. While time is usually the main reason for that, habit is the other. Recently, however, I've made a concerted effort to experience different routes. I'm having such a great time! Sometimes I get lost, but that's generally added fun. I keep my wits about me and stay alert to feelings of danger, and I educate myself as best I can about areas that are too unsafe for exploration. There are so many things to see. I recently found my new favorite dry goods store, too! Now I get my quinoa for $3.00/pound cheaper – all because I was Curious about a different route.

Constructive v. Destructive – I like to look around and decipher for myself all the constructive things I think for myself about a particular situation or thing. Then, I like to look at all the destructive implications. I've done it with jobs, substances, people, garden weeds, spiders, procreation – you name it. Since things/situations/people are rarely all one or the other, this is a fuller way to explore the right path for me. How is this destructive? How is it constructive? Which side outweighs the other? Look around for yourself and be Curious enough to start seeing both sides – and a broader spectrum as a whole.

Write A Story Other-Handed – For years I've noticed exercises in creativity books that ask me to write, "other-handed". Each time I do it I find it an amazing exploration into Body and Mind and their help to the Spirit in finding physical expression. Writing a story other-handed is a fun way to peek into corners of my brain that aren't visible to me normally. As I'm struggling with a hand that isn't adept, I see how my Mind works when the Body isn't. I can't wait each time to see what my story is. What stories are hidden in your other hand? Aren't you Curious to know?

Pixie's Yumspiration
Mushroom Melange

Suggested Ingredients: Mushrooms (as many varieties as are available, preferably fresh, but reconstituted dried works too), **Ghee** (or butter), **Garlic, Shallots, Rosemary, Thyme, Salt, Black Pepper, Balsamic Vinegar**

Preparation: Finely chop garlic and shallots. Clean mushrooms. Chop into small, bite-sized pieces, removing any tough stems. In a skillet, on medium heat, put ghee, garlic, and shallots. Sautee until they become translucent. Add mushrooms, and mix together. Add rosemary, thyme, salt, and pepper. Stir again, reduce heat to low, and cover. Allow mixture to simmer on low – checking to see if it needs to be stirred – for about five minutes, or until mushrooms are soft and fully cooked. Add a splash of balsamic vinegar, stir, cover, turn off heat, and allow to sit for about five minutes before serving. Serve as a side dish. I like it with Jalapeno Kale and a baked potato. Yum!

Consumer Quote: (from a "55-year old woman) "If someone took all the mushrooms, it was me. I'm taking them all. I want them all."

Chapter 2

-Play-

From "Bajour" to Ah-Jour-Bay

My acting career has been fantastic. I'm not yet a "star" or household name, but yet I've had an amazing list of experiences to carry with me along the way. By far the most significantly impactful experience on my resume was the four-year span I was fortunate enough to spend working with Marvin Hamlisch on "Sweet Smell of Success".

In 1998 I was taking class with the awesome Craig Carnelia when he pulled me aside and asked me if I'd like to participate in a reading of a new musical he was penning the lyrics for: "Sweet Smell of Success". The music was written by Marvin Hamlisch, book by John Guare, and directed by Nicholas Hytner – all theatrical royals. The answer was, of course, an easy "yes".

Rehearsals were an incredible trip through the genius mind that was Marvin. He would bound into the rehearsal room several times each day, every time swirling us into laughter and then leaving as impishly as he arrived. We never knew what to expect from him, but we always knew we'd end up in fits of laughter.

Marvin was at work – and so were we – but since composing for the theatre was his favorite job of all, he made sure to savor each moment with all of us, and to share his joy at being able to do what he loved most. What struck me most, though, was Marvin's innate sense of Play. We were his Playmates on his favorite Playground – Broadway – and he made sure to Play with each and every one of us, making each of us feel uniquely special in the process. Every day I sat learning music I eagerly awaited Marvin's arrival so I could have a great laugh.

My favorites among Marvin's games were musical in nature. He could sit at the piano and compose a masterpiece song – lyrics included – at a moment's notice. Or there were the weeks upon weeks during the rehearsals for our all-too-brief Broadway run where Marvin would bound into the room and announce we were going to revive "Bajour" instead of doing "this new stuff". However, since "Bajour" didn't fare well the first time around, he said he had "improved" it by translating the entire score into Pig Latin.

Now the idea itself was funny enough when Marvin presented it, but when he proceeded to sit at the piano and perform his translated pieces, the rooms was in stitches. He had a way of delivering stories and punch lines that produced laughter any professional stand-up comedian would kill for.

But what was he really doing? Reading this, it isn't funny – amusing, maybe – but the hilarity really was born of Marvin's ability to Play with people – any people – and to lighten their burdens for a second. Off and on for four years I had the distinct pleasure of watching Marvin light up a room with his Playful nature.

At the time, though, I didn't personally know how "to Play". I don't remember Playing after the age of 10, when I was first diagnosed with ulcerative colitis. Once I entered into the adult world of Medial Treatments, the little girl I was grew up all too fast and the serious side of life took over. So, by the time I was 28 and sharing space with the Playful Maestro, I was almost two decades away from the concept.

I'd love to say that Marvin's example immediately moved me into action, but it didn't. I simply watched his example, but didn't follow it. I was a "Serious Artist" and there was no time for Play if I wanted to get where I thought I wanted to go in my head.

Subsequent shows followed in the vein of "watch others Play, but don't join. WORK!" There was "Two Gentlemen of Verona" for Shakespeare in the Park where I roller-skated and twirled a jump rope with the seriousness of a Supreme Court Judge. Or "The Pajama Game" with Harry Connick Jr. where I was surrounded by incredibly fun people, but where I could only become bitter and angry when others "stole" my bits. In reality, everyone around me was simply Playing within the Playground of the show. I wasn't. I was *working*.

Or, there was the revival of "Les Mis" where we spent the first week doing impovs but all I could do was huddle off by myself on the edges and protect my space from all the others who where Playing around me. I made it a character choice, so I was doing my job, but I didn't Play and experiment with the rest of my cast. I simply couldn't tap into that part of myself that was open to the vast possibilities that Playing with others can bring. It scared me.

Just before I began my journey with Marvin, I dated a man for a couple of years that began to explore improv while we were together. After his classes, an excited John would come over and try to instill in me the concepts of the Art of Improv that he'd just learned. At its core, there are two that really piggyback off of one another. The first phase he taught me was, "Don't deny. Justify." What? I was raised in the Land of Denial! My trained self was always on the verge of denying that something could be true. And, since I only knew denying, I was certainly a long way from justifying!

The second concept wasn't any easier for me. "Yes. . .And" is an improv actor's first responsibility. Here's how it works: If an actor doing improv says to you, "You're from Fresno, aren't you?", it is your job to answer with an affirmative and something to add to that affirmative – i.e. "Yes, and I love the winters there." Or some other affirming remark. In my world, however, since I wasn't from Fresno, I would have simply answered that actor with, "No, I'm not." And our scene would have been over.

The idea is that where there is "yes....and", there is a possibility of growth, movement, or a fuller storyline. If the answer is "no", there really isn't anywhere to go. And when I was dating John, I was the Queen of scenes (on stage and off) going nowhere on the heels of my continued NO approach to life.

In the wake of shedding all those pounds and their accompanying diseases, I found that the "serious me" that lingered was not so much "me", but a persona I had practiced for so long that I had to relearn the art of Play – or maybe even learn it for the first time.

How does an adult learn such a childish skill? In my case, I needed more Marvins in my life. Tragically at the point I realized this, the Real Marvin Hamlisch passed away unexpectedly. I was sitting in Edinburgh, Scotland when I got the news. I was devastated – to say the least. Marvin had been such an enormous part of my Broadway dreams coming true, and now his amazing, Playful self was gone.

As I sat in Edinburgh, sobbing at the loss of such a person, I decided I would take that beautiful part of him and share it with others – as he had shard it with me. I started practicing Playing everywhere I went. I employed the improv principles John gave me during our time together, and I dove into Playing the Game of Life. With each foray into the arena, I get better and better at it. Often I am fun to Play with, and when I'm not I often hear Marvin's music flooding into my head and it reminds me: Play while I have the time. It may be over far too soon.

How do you Play best? Who do you Play best with? Can you Play with them while you eat some more veg?

Pixie's Rx

Calling All Kids! – Find a fun child (or several) and have a Play Date. Let the child teach you the Art of Play. Whatever they choose (within reason, of course), employ the principle of "Yes...And" and allow it to open the gates to Play. Plus, if it's someone else's child, you've just given them a break in their schedule! They probably needed it. If it's your child, you just grew a great memory to share. Play on!

Game Night – Invite people over for an Adult Game Night. Ask your guests to bring their own games or go on the Internet and research party games to try. Games like Charades and Celebrity don't require anything but Players, so if nobody has an idea, Play one of those. Make a pact that there are no sore winners or losers and enjoy feeling young again.

Monkey Around – Find a public playground near you and spend time on each of the apparatus. Swing with abandon! Move around on the monkey bars! Slide down the slide! Make a hopscotch grid and see if you can win by making it all the way to the highest box! Be merry on the merry-go-ground. Pretend you're ten and have a ball!

Let's Play Pretend – One of my favorite things to do around strangers is to pretend I'm someone else, often with an unidentifiable accent ("I know it's hard to tell where I'm from because I've moved around a lot."). I've been Swedish, British, French, German, a diplomat, deaf, a nun. . . Really anything goes. Just make sure if you're pretending to be deaf on a flight that you don't throw your sister under the bus! ("Kat, how could you pretend that? Now you made me look like a horrible sister for not being able to speak Sign Language with you!") Oops.

Do the Hokey Pokey – I'm not kidding. Sometimes you just need to "turn yourself around – that's what it's all about." Actually, I find the song to be a great physical reminder of how I move through life. I put one part of myself into a situation I take myself out – until my whole self goes in. By the end of a good Hokey Pokey Play I can't help but smile. I can't take credit for the idea (I heard it referenced on TV, but I can't remember for what reason), but I will say my personal Playtime Hokey Pokey is a spectacular performance I am quite proud of.

Collect Something – This does not mean BUY something. Anything can become a collection. Rocks off the side of the road. Sticks fallen from trees. Items found on the sidewalk. Sea glass on a beach. Start looking at the world through the eyes of building your collection. Be a high-end collector. Be choosy about what you allow into your collection and why. Play with different ways to display your collection. Decide who you will invite to see your prizes and why. Take time to devise stories about your items and enjoy the escape from stress as you dive into the world of your treasures.

I Wanna Be Jim Carey – Not literally, but often I park myself in front of my mirror and try to contort my face as brilliantly as he does. I make any funny face I can imagine and I keep at it until I find one that cracks me up. Then, I memorize how it feels in my face, neck, mouth, and heart. I want to remember it so I can use it later, should the need arise. I hope some day to have a Face Off with Mr. Carey!

If I Were Three . . . How Would I Dress Me? – My favorite childhood pictures are ones where I was in charge of my own wardrobe. My choices made no "fashion sense", but if I put myself into my three-year-old mindset, I can see why galoshes, a dress, and a purse worn as a hat make perfect sense. It was summer, but I wanted to jump in puddles and not get my feet wet – or my clothes dirty. It's easy to lift up a dress! And the purse on my head? I might find something to take home during my Playtime! And then I would need a purse! But, until then, I didn't want to carry it around. Now the outfit makes perfect sense! So, go into your closet today. If nobody were judging your combinations, what would you choose to wear? Give yourself a three-year-old fashion show, and maybe clean out your closet as you Play!

Play With Your Food – I know most of our parents asked us not to do this, but I disagree. Playing with the food on my plate allows me to be more present with my meal and better paced with how I consume it. During food preparation, Playing with the food leads me to create delicious dishes. Using my food as a sculptural medium allows me to make beautifully presented food. So, Play away! And enjoy yourself.

Shadows On the Wall – As a little girl when I couldn't sleep I would make up stories about the shadows on my walls. I told myself intricate tales of the grey and white world dancing on my wall. Sometimes, when the moonlight was perfect, I would make my own shadows using my hands and fingers. I could make a bunny, a bird and many "mythological" creatures. Start to notice when there is a shadow Play being presented for you, or schedule to perform one of your own. Dive into the world of your shadows and see what they inspire you to be in the light.

<u>**Pixie's Yumspiration**</u>
Cinnamon Applesauce

Suggested Ingredients: **A Variety of Apples** (Don't choose "delicious" types. Choose tart varieties like Granny Smith, Braeburn or Fuji.), **Cinnamon, Nutmeg, Water, Dried Ginger Root**

Preparation: Wash apples. Remove their peelings,(You can bake those in the oven with some butter, cinnamon and nutmeg for delicious snacks.), core, and cut into small pieces. In a saucepan, put about an inch of water in the bottom. Turn burner to medium heat. Put apples into water. Bring to a boil, stirring constantly. Add spices to taste. Reduce heat to simmer, stir, and cover pot. Allow to simmer until apples are completely softened. Once fully cooked (and slightly cooled), place into a food processor for final pureeing. Serve warm or cold.

Consumer Quote: (from a 48-year old woman) "Nothing makes me feel better than your applesauce."

Chapter 3
-Career-

No More Hiding

I am one of those people who always knew what my dream Career was – and I was certain I would achieve that dream: To Be On Broadway. I recently got a Facebook message from a high school teacher of mine that said: "I can distinctly remember you talking about going to NY and performing and I was like.....OK. Well you showed me. Good for you! Glad to see your dream came true."

I loved getting that message. It was the validation a young girl had sought out many years ago each time she would step on stage or tell someone her Giant Dream. And while I'm now no longer in need of the approval of others where my Career is concerned, it was a nice "atta-girl" to store away now that I'm beginning my second Career – with even loftier goals than my first Career contained. I loved receiving the reminder that naysayers will be all around me, and that's ok. It doesn't reflect on the validity of my dreams. I just dream differently than some others I meet and come to know.

My first Big Dream – to work on Broadway – came true so many times I lost count. Of course, as I learned more about the "Business of Broadway", my dream became refined further to include nuances such as; to be an Original Cast Member, to perform on the Tonys, and to be in a Tony Award winning show as an original cast member. With each new dream, I loved achieving it and setting the next rung on the Career ladder for myself.

By the time I was a vacation swing in "Mary Poppins", though, my fervor for my Broadway Career was starting to become worn down. At the end of three-and-a-half-years of multiple stints in both the Broadway and National Touring Companies, I found myself hiding behind a potted tree in front of a Starbucks in Portland, Oregon. I was avoiding the resident director. In my ear I heard Mary Poppins herself speak to my soul saying, "Spit Spot! Why would an adult need to hide behind a potted tree?! Tidy up your world so you can walk with your shoulders back and your head held high! Really! A potted tree?!"

Mary was right. Why was a 41-year-old woman hiding like a child? The answer wasn't enjoyable – nor easy – for me to voice: I had allowed my Career goals to become smaller and smaller and smaller without noticing I'd done so – and the result was that I was hiding from a man whom I had allowed to make me feel small time and time again. I had lost sight of MY CAREER – and how I wanted that to look – and was instead focusing on having a JOB.

Working with the man in charge of keeping "Mary Poppins" running was a continually worsening situation for me. I enjoyed each performance with immense pleasure. Off the cuff comments I might be subjected to each day by the resident director, however, were another story. My life had become an exhausting exercise of looking around every corner in the theatre like a cat on a hunt – so that if I saw him I could run away undetected and find a different route to take, or hide out of sight until he passed by.

That was the culture this man had created. There were two camps: Those he adored and treated beautifully; and those he slowly tortured into hiding in the shadows so we wouldn't receive his blows that day. I took solace in the fact that I wasn't alone – that others confessed to me they too were hiding in the folds of the curtains or jumping behinds set pieces just as often as I had done. Instead of asking myself why I was ok with being in the Hiders Club, I simply swallowed my pain, faked niceties when I couldn't avoid him, and concentrated on enjoying the days when he wasn't at the theatre.

The uncanny part, however, was that he ALWAYS seemed to be where I was, which was odd to me. I came in and out of the two companies, one that was constantly moving! For some reason, however, whenever I was under contract he was there – usually for the entirety of my stay. I started to become obsessed with that fact. I knew he was also responsible for other big shows – shows that I thought might need his attention! But with each contract and then appearance of him, I marveled at the improbability. So by the time I went to Portland, Oregon on a six-day contract over the fourth of July week, I viewed his arrival on the morning of mine to be a sign that this was the last time I should ever say yes to another "Mary Poppins" contract. It was time for me to go.

But go where? Wait for another Broadway show to come my way? After years of experiencing long runs, reaching all the goals I had set (except for two), and feeling frustrated at repeating the same story for longer than I enjoyed, I didn't want to put all my energy into the same direction. I also didn't want to completely abandon Broadway when I still have two goals to reach. And, I didn't want to start a life where I suffered through a JOB each day, hoping one day retirement would save me.

So I started to ask myself questions. What do I like to do? What impact do I want my Career to have on the world? How do I want my work life to look? Who do I want surrounding me as I work? What hidden talents do I have? What Career path could I carve out for myself? With each new question came more new questions and after months of searching, I found my way. I've developed a new Career path for myself, and given myself a new title: Ambassador of the Art of Healthy Living. I love my new Career. And I love being the one who is defining it.

Recently a close family member wanted to impart some wisdom upon me: I am applying for a job that doesn't exist. I loved hearing that phrase launch out toward me. Yes! I'm on the right path! I now have naysayers to show the way to! I believe with hard work and persistence I can achieve whatever I desire. My past 43 years have taught me this is true because my story speaks for itself. I not only reached my goal to be on Broadway, I've stayed there for over 20 years. And that story came true because each day, week, month, and year I kept pressing on. With every setback I concentrated on getting past it so I could reach my desired destination.

My new Career is larger than my old one by far! Especially given that the old one is a large component of the new one! The Broadway community is my home and now that I'm here, I'm not moving away. However, as Ambassador of the Art of Healthy Living, I enjoy travelling far and wide and sharing Broadway with those who haven't been as fortunate to have it as their home. As Ambassador, I can spread the beautiful world that is Broadway to tons of others...and hopefully inspire others to dream higher than just having a J.O.B. Make your own Career! Give yourself a great title, and enjoying creating your own Empire. Oh, and make it a rule that many vegetables will be eaten there!

Pixie's Rx

Everyone's An Entrepreneur – I fully believe everyone has an idea for the "Perfect Business". As humans we have the opportunity to create our own life – and business is a large part of this life creation. If I have a business idea now, I go after it. I can't know what is – or isn't – a viable business opportunity unless I'm willing to invest myself in the process of exploring it. Just recently a new business idea of mine just netted me $625.00! Create your own businesses – large or small – and see where your Career might go!

"What Do You Want to Be When You Grow Up?" – As a child I remember so many people asking this question of me or other kids around me. I also remember the answers being things like "a princess and a nurse" or "a fireman and a doctor." The questioning adults always laughed and said something like, 'Well you'll have to choose one! You can't be both!' WHY NOT??!! Grace Kelly was a famous actress AND a princess. In my case I wanted to be a Broadway actress and a healer. At the crossroads of my Broadway career I reread an old diary where I had stated those two desires to my "Dear Kitty". I had forgotten I had wanted to heal others as an active profession. To date I'm working toward this new Career with passion and under the wise counsel of the Bible that says in Luke, "Physician, heal thyself." And so far, this directive is serving me well. What did your "small self" dream of being? By entertaining the dream – or an adult version of it – can you shift to a new profession that will bring you joy?

Row, Row, Row Your Boat, Gently Down the Multiple Streams - ...of Income, that is. What are you good at that could help you to generate an additional stream of income? As an actress I've had to master this skill in order to stay afloat in NYC. Do you have a craft you could sell on Etsy? Are you a fast typist who could work from home? Do you have items around your home that you could up-cycle into moneymakers? Are you someone who spots "gems" at garage and estate sales? Maybe those "finds" could turn into a great online antique business. When you generate an additional stream of income from a small investment of time or in conjunction with an activity you already enjoy, you can help yourself start to break free from a Career that has become unsatisfying for whatever reason. Or maybe you'd just like more money to spend on vacation!

Facebook Forum – Start to ask questions on Facebook or other chat sites. Things like; "What is your favorite aspect of your job (other than pay)?" "When you look at your Career, how does it satisfy you?" "Whose Career do you find most interesting, and why?" "What businesses do you wish were in your current living area?" By brainstorming with others, we can find ourselves open to a whole lot of great ideas that spark other great ideas. Look to keep the questions phrased in a positive manner, and phrased to be more than "yes" or "no" answers. Some people's Careers will really surprise you. It's a big world out there filled with many people who feel satisfied in their work lives. Ask them how they manage to achieve that when you come across one. Allow the inspiration of others to help be your new Career counselor.

How Can I Serve My Community? – One of the greatest networking tools I have ever found is through work I've done to better my community. Being in an environment where people feel positively about how they are spending their time helps to allow openness and generosity to flow. I've also met people from professions very far away from mine, which has opened my eyes to many new ideas and thoughts of how to build "My Empire". In the process, I get to make a positive impact on my world and get to know the people who live around me in it. I feel safer knowing more of my community and it's fun to walk down the streets and be greeted warmly by those who I've shared my time volunteering with . . .and it's gotten me jobs that gave me help with my Career(s)!

"I'm Stuck Here! I Can't Change My Career!" – While this one is disheartening, it's not hopeless. There are so many ways in which we can improve even the hardest work environments. For those in stressful, 'I can't show emotion' jobs, we can still pause for a minute and do mindfulness practices. Just a minute pause here and there becomes of great benefit to your whole self. In my situation, I was stuck in a job for a few years that was really hard on me physically, emotionally, AND mentally. And I wasn't in a position to quit. So I made my time there entertaining to me by doing silly things like dusting myself in glitter for the enjoyment of myself, and others. I noticed I got yelled at less when coated in Pixie Dust! I also chose to smile when I was there, and to think one kind thing about every person I saw. While it was still necessary for me to leave that job in order for me to resume my "Career", I was able to truly tolerate my time there – and some of it was even fun.

The Billings LaPierre Principle – One of my "secret weapons" I learned early on in my Career. After my sophomore year in college I wanted to do Summer Stock. I researched my options and I chose my target – Maine State Music Theatre. I travelled to NYC for their apprentice auditions, sang for the Artistic Director, Victoria Crandall, and went back to college in Boston. After a week of hearing nothing I called the theatre to inquire. I was put on the phone with a man with a kind voice. "Hi!" I chirped. "I auditioned for your apprentice program last week, and, well, you're my first choice, so I was wondering if you've scheduled callbacks yet?" "We're a bit behind this year, I'm afraid. Can you call back next week?" I did. I chirped my hello again. Again the kind man asked me to call back, now in a few days. This scene repeated itself two more times before the kind voice said, "You're hired!" on the fifth phone call. Later that

24

summer, after the kind voice and I knew one another as people he said, "Two hours after you initially auditioned Victoria Crandall died. I had no idea who you were when you called, but I liked your persistence and sunny "Hello" so I followed my gut and let you come. I'm glad I did. You're one of the best apprentices we've ever had." That kind man was Billings LaPierre. Never give up. Kind persistence pays off. (So does kind acceptance. Billings got a great apprentice twice as a result . . . and now he has a Principle named after him! I wonder how he feels about that...)

Befriend the Benefit of "No" – One of the greatest things being an actress has taught me is the benefit of receiving a "no". As humans we don't like to hear "NO", but I know most of us have a proclivity to say "no" very quickly – a la when it was one of the first words we learned while being raised by our families. "NO" is meant to be a teacher when we are young. It's meant to set a barrier and a boundary. It seems limiting. But as the years go along, many of us are re-taught that we are obligated to say "yes" when something is requested of us; which makes hearing "no" all the tougher. I have found, though, that learning to say "NO" again – with kindness and in a timely manner – has been incredibly beneficial to growing my Career in the way I envision it today. Conversely, hearing "NO" is a time saver for me now, instead of a barrier. If I receive a "NO" now? I assess what made that the perfect answer for today, and I move along, benefitting from whatever I've learned. Also, I don't believe the "NO" always means "Never". Things change.

Punishment v. Protection – The greatest Career-boosting idea I've learned is how to bounce back after disappointment. One of my favorite ways is to use the mantra "I'm not being punished, I'm being protected." Or, "I didn't lose anything . . . I'm only getting' something greater later! If I dwelled on every Career "disappointment", I'd never get out there and try again. I need to have ways to look at not getting a job that are helpful and productive for me. I don't get A LOT of the jobs I "apply" for. As an actress, that's a fairly normal statement. And, because I have to invest myself into each attempt, I need to be able to un-invest just as well. So, find ways to speak to yourself that builds your ability to dismount and proudly walk way. Keeping in mind protection is always ours.

Get Paid to Play – I've had hundreds of jobs in my lifetime. I've worked in the corporate world, creative world, and many worlds in between. What I've found is that jobs where I can incorporate "play" feel like heaven. Jobs where it's all serious work are tough for me to show up to – especially with joy. In all sectors are jobs that allow play. Looking to work in such a manner has allowed me to keep finding meaningful ways to advance my Career. I often say, "Where there is play lives a short, fun day. Where there is only work – depression fully lurks!" Find a way to play in your Career. There are enough depressed people in our workforce already!

Pixie's Yumspiration
Rainbow Quinoa

Suggested Ingredients: Red, White, and Black Quinoa, Walnuts, Dried Apricots, Fresh Blueberries and Raspberries, Cinnamon, Nutmeg, Maple Syrup

Preparation: Chop walnuts and apricots into small pieces. In a pan, boil water for quinoa (2 parts water to one part quinoa). Once it is boiling, add quinoa, walnuts, apricots, cinnamon, and nutmeg. Stir just to incorporate ingredients. Cover pot and reduce heat to simmer. Simmer for 20 minutes. Scoop quinoa mixture into a bowl and top with fresh berries and a drizzle of maple syrup.

Consumer Quote: (from Joy Bauer on the Today Show) "It's out of this world."

Chapter 4
-Health-

The Fat Lady is Done Singing

I love to sing. I've ALWAYS loved to sing. I remember my first public performance at the age of 3. My sister claims that she was standing beside me and I didn't so much sing, as play with my prop. That's not how I remember it! I remember that I sang a song called "The B-I-B-L-E". (This also correlates to the first two words I learned to spell: Bible and Blood. Yikes!) What I vividly remember loving was standing on the "stage", seeing everyone pay rapt attention to me. It was pure magic. And from that first taste of life on stage, I wanted more.

When my career on Broadway really took off, though, my Health was in serious decline. I was quite obese, I had ulcerative colitis, plantar fasciitis, asthma, chronic bronchitis, extreme depression, intense anxiety, and a whole other list of ailments. I was falling apart from the inside out – which was making my dream of being on stage in front of others become a horrible nightmare. I spent all of my performances unable to even enjoy the accolades of the audience at the end of a number or a show. I was too busy catching my breath – trying to appear like I wasn't winded – or simply wishing the applause would end so I could go home and sit down and self-medicate.

By the time I did the revival of "The Pajama Game" with Harry Connick, Jr. on Broadway, I was a crumbling person. My physical Health was always precarious, as was my mental Health. Most days I was just trying to hold on . . . and usually failing before the night's end. I felt completely trapped by my ill Health, but unable to do much about it.

By the end of the run of that show I wasn't functioning. I picked fights with people or became the "tragic victim" of

28

another's behavior. My joints were killing me, I napped every spare second I could, I avoided being naked or allowing people to touch me. I had my inhalers waiting in either wing, dressing room, and with the wardrobe supervisor. I cried – sometimes for days – and couldn't stop completely, even when on stage. All my systems were failing and my life had become a chore to live. Not even singing gave me escape or joy. Trying to sing simply reminded me how unhealthy I had become.

When that show closed and I had a minute to rest and regroup, I started to truly understand that if I wanted a different life, I had to address my Health first. I knew I needed to figure out where it had all gone wrong and to try to repair damage caused from years of complete disregard of my physical Health, which I believe completely eroded my mental Health – which, in turn, started to annihilate my spirit. No matter what way I sliced it for myself, if I didn't start by first taking care of my physical self, my mental and spiritual selves would have no hope of survival.

When had this all begun for me? I knew that in order to truly cure an ailment I had to trace it to its causal issue. What had caused me to be *so* ill for so long? When I told my life story in brief it was overwhelmingly filled with stories of sicknesses, surgeries, illnesses, medications, procedures and lists of doctors in various specialties. At the age of thirty-six my life story could be boiled down to one of sickness and the drama that sickness brings along with it. Once I could boil it down that simply I saw that the story didn't begin with me. I was raised to be this way.

There is zero blame in that last phrase, by the way. My family has given me more support and such amazing life gifts that I consider myself truly blessed to have them as "mine". But the truth is, by the time I was in-utero, my 30-year-old father was quite ill. By the time I was four months old he had had his first open heart surgery. As this was 1971, this was no small surgery. My father's recovery was brutal and decades later his scars still marked him with a vividness that seemed impossible after so many decades.

As a baby I spent much of my time in bed with my father. He recovered and I grew. And as I grew, I became very sick, very young. I was following in my father's footsteps, not understanding that I was. And, since my adult-sized illness began at age ten, when I sat retracing how I had gotten to be so very ill by the age of thirty-six, it was no surprise. I simply followed in my parents' footsteps like many children do. They were my main teachers and I was a good student.

Eventually I needed to look at what else had they taught me that I could follow instead. As I looked at this idea with enormous desire to find answers, almost immediately I realized they taught me to be curious as to how things worked. My father was a good mechanic and constantly sought to understand how different engines functioned. My mom is a mathematician and loves to find strings of numbers that have a cool pattern or a way in which nature and math are inextricably intertwined.

On the heels of curiosity, I realized they had taught me the immense importance of education. My mother is an educator, and has been her entire adult life. My father was a voracious student, constantly studying different subjects, memorizing facts and figures and seeking to understand things on a deeply comprehended level. My parents paid for my education and still to this day send me money to help pay for classes I am taking.

And I also realized they taught me about Health and the importance of good nutrition. My father passed away just a week ago, which is terribly hard to believe. He lived much longer than anyone ever expected, though, and I believe that was in large part because of the way he nourished his body all those years. I can't remember a day of my life growing up where I didn't see my father eating vegetables. He loved them and ate them all day, every day. He wasn't a vegetarian – far from it – but a large portion of his diet was always vegetables. Even when his doctor advised him to eat less of them because the vitamin K clotted his blood too much (he had an artificial heart valve), my father simply asked his doctor to please raise the dose of anticoagulant to accommodate his love of veg. I remember at the time I thought he was nuts. The doctor had given him permission to eat junk food! But my father took care of himself with veg instead.

As I began to see these other well-taught lessons unfold in front of me, I became focused on turning myself around and learning to care for my body and be curious about how I could best accomplish my goal. I educated myself about nutrition, even getting trained as a Health Coach in the process. And I started to eat my veg every day. And while I still have improvements I want to make to my Health even today, the exciting news is that I no longer get sick. I haven't had even so much as a sniffle in years. Other than the rare seasonal allergy here and there, I am well 100% of the time.

Well, physically well. The mental and spiritual Health also needed to be helped, but for those I have needed to look outside just what my family taught me. (This may spark some anger in people, but this is just my personal story. I'm not saying this is true for all people.) I feel my mental illnesses largely correlated to my physical disregard. When my diet consisted of all processed food, I was crazy. There isn't any other word for it. I was simply crazy. And now it makes total sense to me. My brain didn't have a chance in hell to be stable given the poor quality of fuel it was receiving by me all day, every day. I was eating myself crazy. And now I eat myself sane. I feed my brain consciously so that I can remain a sane participant in my life – not beholden to a malfunctioning organ that I was actively making nonfunctional.

Once I experienced Health in my physical self, addressed my mental self and soothed that, and looked around to see if I was yet "Healthy", I recognized I still had a very sickly part of myself to attend to: My Spirit. I hadn't thought about that part of myself in years, and it was showing in the form of unexplained ennui and overall boredom of life. I recognized that without the Spirit getting its share of care, I would still watch Health elude me.

But how to take care of a part of me I'd forgotten needed attention? I searched for when I had left it behind. And I nurtured my Spirit at that age – the age it stopped growing. So now I can take care of my Spirit in many ways. My favorite way is singing. If I don't sing often, my Spirit shrivels and starts to get sick. I'm grateful I live in a time and a place where I get to sing whenever I want to. It's a gift that allows me to be able to be the Healthy woman I now am. And, just to care for my Spirit further, I am nurturing many other things that make my Spirit soar so I will always have a choice of medicines.

What can you do to heal your Mind, Body, *and* Spirit so you can have full and awesome Health? What gifts have you been given that you aren't yet using? How could those gifts be medicines for you today? How many veg have you eaten today?

Pixie's Rx

Solo Twister – Growing up in the 70s and 80s I was exposed to some awesome games. One of my absolute favs was Twister – but I liked to play it by myself. I liked to see if I could move from one contorted position to another with grace and ease. The first experience I had with yoga felt like a better-honed version of my Solo Twister games, which made it more like a play date with myself rather than an activity meant to "be Healthy". But yoga is incredibly Healthy. Focusing, breathing, stretching, holding, twisting, and strengthening are several of the many benefits it provides. However, for me, I need a fun reason to do something and pretending that I'm playing Solo Twister instead of "being Healthy" keeps me coming back for more.

I Talk to the Trees – I grew up in The Sticks of Ohio where woods were plentiful, and a great place to lose myself for a day. I would hang out on warm spring days, searching for wildflowers and spider webs, bird's nests, and fairies. I never knew there was a culture that had a term for my Healthy playtime. In Japan they call it shinrin-yoku, which translates literally to "forest bathing". In recent years several studies have emerged stating the benefits of walking in the woods – or amongst any nature. Scientists are confirming what I knew instinctively as a little girl – Mother Nature has all sorts of free stuff that can keep us Healthy if we just take the time to use it! So, go outside! See some nature. Walk around in it. Bathe in a forest or two. Hug a few trees and tell them your problems. Studies have shown that trees emit "wood-essential oils" that have all kinds of Health benefits, including a decrease in depression. I'll take that over a pill or a visit to a shrink any day!

As Marvin Gaye Did Say – Sexual healing is one of the Healthiest things you can do for yourself. I grew up in a religion that wanted to define sexuality for me, which caused a fair amount of physical and mental issues for me when I found my sexual Health existed outside the parameters given to me as a child. I encourage everyone to go inward and come to a loving understanding of what sexual Health is for you. It is an entirely different picture for each and every person who walks this earth. It can't be defined by anyone outside of the individual because no two people live the exact same story. And who I have been as a sexual creature is constantly evolving and changing as I evolve and change. What was appropriate for my sexual Health has not remained fixed throughout my 44 years. Given that fact, I don't believe my definition of sexuality for myself – and definitely not others – should be forced to be fixed either. Find your own path to sexual Health. And love yourself as you walk it.

Mine Your Mind – The best way to live a Healthy life is through your own power and vision. When others are guiding your journey it may go along ok for a while, but eventually that time will come where a voice somewhere inside of you speaks up and says, "uh, uh!" In our culture we are taught to ignore that voice, but it is, in fact, your instinct talking. It is trying to help keep you safe and alive. It's not a pushy voice, and it often gently speaks, allowing for small shifts to happen that alter trajectories away from terror just enough to avert total disaster. The best way to hone this voice's efficacy is through simple meditation. Choose to go inward with regularity and watch your instinctive voice grow stronger and more helpful in supporting you to be your Healthiest you.

Start With the Garnish – One of the silliest things we humans do is to avoid taking even the simplest good care of ourselves. The only undisputed fact in the vast world of nutrition is that we should EAT VEGETABLES! We can't agree on anything other than that, so let's start there. If you aren't a veg eater today, consciously become one starting your next meal. No matter where you are eating, if there is a veg served to you, eat it first. Your only rule to Health here is that you have to clean your plate of veg. First. It's amazing how just looking for veg on my plate – first – shifts my perspective on what I'm actually doing when I eat. I am nourishing myself first off . . . so I eat my veg first and fully. If all you get is a pickle and a garnish of kale, make sure you eat that kale! All two bites!

Masticate What's On Your Plate – Next time you go out to eat, look around at the diners surrounding you. How many times do they chew each bite of food? Do they finish one bite before starting on the next? Do they fill their mouths with food and then wash it down by gulping a beverage? I was amazed when I started to watch others eat . . . and then notice my own no-chew patterns. It turns out that chewing is a really great idea if you'd like good digestion, Health, and a smaller waistline. While I personally dislike counting the number of chews I successfully complete, I DO like envisioning myself having an awesome food transforming factory working inside of my skin. The first department is "Chaos and Assimilation". The first few chews create chaos, but that's only half the job. The second set of chews create assimilation, which is essential in order for chaos to not be the energy flowing through the rest of my factory for the next day or more. Whatever you need to do to remind yourself to chew....Do! And Chew, Chew, Chew....

Ritualistic Like Rainman – In the movie "Rainman" Dustin Hoffman's character ritualistically repeats certain phrases. Simple things like; "go slow on the driveway", and listing his timetable of activities for the afternoon. Repeating these phrases and knowing how his day would lay out were comforting and soothing to Rainman. I, too, am comforted and soothed by rituals, schedules, and easy phrases that help me to remember certain Health "rules" that work for me. Things like when I look at an item of food, my first question is always, "Does this fit me or fat me?" Additionally, I start my day out in the same order each day, which helps me feel anchored and ready to face what might pop up next! Rituals help us to return to our present self. And they are also very soothing. Ask Rainman!

Become A Stress Ball . . . Not A Ball of Stress – I love those little stress balls that doctors give out to help ease carpal tunnel syndrome. I don't love them for that purpose, but I love how resilient they are. For the record, yoga and acupuncture helped me more than the stress balls, but I digress. Anyway, I love how those rubbery balls immediately return to its original form, no matter how hard it's squeezed. I think of my own resiliency level often. How easily do I bounce back? Studies show that learning to become resilient can help to lower stress significantly. In my own personal study, I would say I feel like human proof that that's true. In what ways can you learn to bounce back quickly?

Lovingly Evict the Destructive Addict – I know very few people who aren't addicted to something destructive these days – myself included. Our culture is set up to lure you to something harmful when overused, and then it hooks you into over-using it. Then, as a society, we shame those who become addicts. I have found that that model is one of the unhealthiest ones we've embraced as a society. Instead I embrace my addictive self, but I lovingly make my world uninhabitable for those addictions that are costing me too much. I work to slowly change my habits and patterns in order to disrupt the rut that destructive addictions cause. I don't go cold turkey usually, although I have. However you can evict the destructive addict – do it! Then flaunt your new, healthy addictions that come to stay instead.

Always Take Your Zzzzzs – Get enough sleep. Period. Nothing pithy here. Just get enough sleep. It's non-negotiable. No sleep = No Health. Get. Enough. Sleep!

Pixie's Yumspiration
Jalapeno Kale

Suggested Ingredients: Kale (any type, although lacinto is my favorite), **Bacon** (2 strips per bunch of kale), **Shallots** (or onions), **Garlic**, **Olive Oil** (if needed if bacon doesn't produce enough grease), **Balsamic Vinegar**, **Pickled Jalapenos**, **Cumin**, **Salt**, **Pepper**

Preparation: Wash kale, making sure to remove all soil from leaves. Set aside in colander to drain a bit. Chop shallots and garlic to desired size. I like them finely chopped. Chop bacon strips into quarter-inch sized strips. On stovetop place skillet, and turn burner up to medium-high heat. Put bacon, shallots and garlic into the pan and sauté until shallots start to become translucent, and bacon fat does too. If not a lot of bacon fat produced, add a bit of olive oil. Next, chop kale into bite-sized pieces and add to pan. Turn heat down to low. Sprinkle cumin, salt, and pepper to taste. Stir all together and cover pan for about a minute or two. Next, add pickled jalapenos – either chopped or whole – to taste, and a splash of balsamic vinegar. Stir, cover and simmer for another minute or two, until kale stems are fork tender.

Consumer Quote: (from an 8-year old boy) "I don't know what my mom is talking about! Good-for-you-food doesn't have to taste bad! Can I have more jalapeno kale please?"

Chapter 5
-Exercise-

Let's Get Physical –
Let Your Body Talk!

One of the most frequent questions I am asked is, "What do you do for Exercise?" People are always shocked at the answer. Nobody can believe that I lost 100 pounds AND have maintained that weight loss without being tethered to the gym all day, six days a week. Shows like "The Biggest Loser" have conditioned us to think that if we've allowed ourselves to become fat, the punishment is purgatory where personal trainers screaming at us is the new daily life experience.

The truth is, weight loss AND maintenance is 80% about what you eat, 10% genetics, and 10% is dependent upon Exercise. I didn't know those percentages until just a year ago, but in my experience they are totally accurate. When I was regularly dancing on Broadway and as "Mrs. Claus" for Radio City, I was getting sometimes hours of strenuous Exercise each and every day – but I wasn't thin. In fact, the more I danced in shows, the fatter I got – largely because the increased Exercise made me hungrier than I was used to so I ate more – telling myself with each bite that I was "working it off", so it was ok.

While all the Exercising I have done was great for my cardiovascular health, overall flexibility, and muscle tone, it's not really a weight-loss tool in my humble opinion. Exercise, for me, is a way to keep my Mind and Spirit in the game WITH my Body – not ignoring it and "pushing through the pain", for instance.

As a kid I never focused on Exercise until my teen years when my weight came into the forefront due to the influence of fashion magazines, TV stars, and the opinions of other people based upon how they felt I SHOULD look. Before that I "Exercised" for fun, something to do, or to master a physical skill like a walkover or the splits. I rode my bike for hours each week, not to burn calories, but to be able to go see friends and play together. At that point my body wasn't in need of "correction". It just needed to move or to go someplace.

As I embarked on my weight loss in 2006, I decided I didn't want to join ANOTHER gym. How many thousands of dollars had I paid to those companies, only to never or rarely go? Because, in truth, I hated it. I hated the unnatural lighting, the smell of others' sweat, and the way doing stationary Exercises made me feel stagnant, stuck, and sometimes "stupid". I'd be on a treadmill running at 6.0 thinking 'This sucks! If I'm going this fast I should be getting somewhere!'.

With no gym, though, what would work? I thought back to my mother's journey with her weight. When she was 40, just about the age I was then, she lost a ton of weight simply by altering her diet and WALKING! Outside. Every day. That was it. She would walk "around the block", which was actually a four-mile trek across the country roads surrounding her home. The summer I came back from college with the "Freshman Fifteen" (more like forty!) on me, she "required" I take those walks with her.

At the time I truly resented it, but I am immensely grateful now, as those walks and her example showed me how effective such an easy action can be. Even in my surliness at the time, the walks always made me feel better and I loved breathing in all the smells in the air and the sights all around. Being at the gym I received neither benefit.

So I decided to walk again in 2006. I committed to thirty minutes each day, but allowed myself to do it in five-minute increments to start. I walked outside, taking in my environment, and learning more about it with every step. I live in the New York City area, so walking is incredibly easy for me to enjoy with all the paths and sidewalks around me. With each step I not only moved back into my body, but I moved into my city as well.

Over six years later, walking is the only consistent Exercise I employ. I wish I walked every day, but sometimes scheduling, weather, or travel prohibits me from getting out there and enjoying myself. At this point, if I have too many days like that in a row I become like a caged animal. I NEED to walk. Without it my joints start to get sore, my spirit sags, and my mind shifts into a strange kind of hyper-drive that makes me feel a bit crazy.

Ultimately, I don't feel it matters WHAT kind of Exercise you do. It only matters that you DO it. And consistently. Not to lose weight – or to keep it off – but because your body NEEDS it. Our sedentary society goes against the primal need our body has to be in motion. For centuries Exercise was a way of life for existence. It STILL is, but we often don't see its necessity until things like obesity, arthritis, or other illnesses come to play.

One of the greatest benefits of being on Broadway was being introduced to people who LIVE fully inside their bodies. Professional dancers are truly high-level athletes and watching them work their magic up close is incredible. I got to see how they lived and worked within their bodies and what things were across the board consistent in how they maintain such physical prowess.

First of all, the majority of them ate extremely well. Vegetables are staples in many of their diets and I learned a great deal about portion size from seeing their meal portions. I'm not saying all dancers are the "picture of health", but so many of them are that I had truly inspirational examples all around me to learn from. I know I had a unique set of "teachers" around me, and now I'm happy to share their wisdom with those who aren't fortunate enough to be behind those awesome Stage Doors.

In addition to their food choices, I noticed that the dancers I admired also stretched before (and sometimes after) each rehearsal or show. They seemed to enjoy it and it always looked like it felt so good that I started to add a bit of that into my life, too. And then I heard them talking about the "magic" of yoga. Many, many dancers have consistent yoga practices that help to keep them strong, limber, and as physically balanced as one can get. I'd see them coming in from classes – glowing and radiating joy. Their example got me on the yoga mat to find out for myself.

I strive to do more yoga. I very rarely get myself on the mat these days, but when I do I love how I feel. Old injuries start to heal and my anxiety levels lessen. But, as I'm not a girl who likes to Exercise for hours and hours each week, I stay with my favorite – walking – and add in other things when I feel like it.

Whatever your favorite type of Exercise is, make it a consistent part of your schedule. I work my walk into my commute into The City. If I leave just fifteen minutes "early" I can walk two miles to the ferry or to the last bus stop before the tunnel and I'm done for the day. I love how that time helps me to organize myself and – like bathing, eating, sleeping and other self-care actions – it's now just a part of my happy, healthy life.

What Exercise makes you happy? Where do you prefer to Exercise? Do you prefer to do it alone or with a buddy? How can you gently add Exercise to your self-care routine every day? Maybe you can take a walk to the store to buy some veg! Then make sure you eat those veggies – and burn some calories chewing!

Pixie's Rx

Finding Five – Keeping your muscles strong is important for bone and joint health as well as maintaining your metabolism and remaining healthy into old age. Frailty is one of the biggest precursors to sickness and death. So, I focus upon maintaining the muscles I've got. For five minutes, a couple of times a week, I do a combination of at-home strength training Exercises, using my body as my weight system. Try using a combination of the following and then add some of your own: Plank, Triceps Dips, Wall Sits, Jumping Jacks, Deep Knee Bends, V-Seats, etc. (You can easily find examples of each Exercise on the internet.)

Dance Like No One Is Looking – I love to dance, but unless I'm following choreography I don't produce movements that anyone would want to pay to watch. However, when I'm home alone I often like to put on music that moves or stimulates me, and I DANCE! I use my home as my Broadway set and I become the solo dancer I always wanted to be in my dreams. And the best part of all is that it's amazing cardiovascular Exercise, it helps to tone my whole body, and afterward I get an endorphin rush that helps propel me onto the next task of my day. Just one song has enormous benefits. And often I enjoy a nude ballet or modern piece – just for fun! I imagine exuberant applause as my dance commences… and I enjoy taking a bow!

Dance Party – Along the same lines as dancing solo, but a totally different experience, is being part of an actual dance party. It doesn't have to be fancy. I've had great ones with just an iPhone, a few feet of space, and two friends, that have left awesome memories – and no doubt some of my sweat on some rugs! Dance until you are breathless, then put on a ballad and slow yourself down. Then crank it back up again. Whatever you want, but DANCE, DANCE, DANCE! Trade "signature moves" and enjoy being goofy with others AND getting great Exercise to boot!

Gallop, Gallop, Skip, Skip – "Kids activities" like galloping and skipping are really fun ways to get your heart rate up and your legs toned – in a very short time. Have you ever tried to gallop a mile? Or skip for ten minutes straight? Those are extreme workouts in my book! A marathon seems like nothing compared to skipping for more than a few yards. Just a few minutes of alternating these two kid steps and you'll be done with your workout in no time.

Make Your House Shine Like the Top Of the Chrysler Building! – I always wanted to be in the musical "Annie" as a kid. Most women my generation who loved musicals wanted to be "Annie", I have found. Although that never happened for me, I can still pretend like Miss Hannigan is yelling at me as I scrub my own floors. When my floors look great, so do my arms and shoulders and back and abs. Get into cleaning your home old school – like the orphans did. Scrub those floors; wash those walls. Tone your body while you make your home fit for the royalty you are about to become once Daddy Warbucks comes along!

Sexercise (Orgasmic Isometrics) – In whatever way you enjoy sex in your life, have it! Get into your body as you like to and see how your enjoyment changes when you clench and hold certain muscles at one time. Try holding your quadriceps or glutes for a few seconds. Feel the rush of relief as you release them. Find your way to physical ecstasy and tone your abs, arms, butt, and legs in the process. You can also use sex as great cardio vascular Exercise, if you choose. Work up a sweat while you're raising other beneficial hormones resulting from sex. Think you feel great after one or the other? Combine the two with intent and enjoy the free ride!

From the "Gated Community" – I used to have a boss at a corporate job who used to be a prison guard prior to his position "guarding" billionaires' financial secrets. He would often regale us with stories from what I like to refer to as "The Gated Community". Many of Tony's tips were extremely useful – like "10 to 1s". Tony taught me the most popular cardio workout for inmates during his tenure as a guard. All you need is a space to stand at full height and a few inches above your head. If you have enough space to hold your arms out in front of you, stick those babies out! Stand up. Jump 10 times in place. Turn to your left one-quarter of a turn. Jump 10 more times. Turn another quarter turn to your left. Jump 10. Turn one more quarter, jump 10. Turn back to the start. Repeat with 9, 8, 7, etc. – down to 1. Great sweat and quad workout!

The Elevator Is Broken – I noticed at one point just how many escalators and elevators I encountered in a day. Were they all necessary? I made a two-part rule for myself: First, if there are four flights or less, I take the stairs. The second part of the rule states that if I'm not carrying anything, I JOG up the stairs. Over the course of a week I do many flights of steps now. And my legs and butt thank me for it.

Get On Your Feet – And WALK. JUST WALK. With purpose, and aim for at least 30 minutes a day…. but JUST WALK. The only consistent Exercise I've done throughout losing 100 pounds and keeping it off has been walking. JUST GO WALK.

Hike, Hike Baby! – Great in all ways is hiking. It works your legs, your core, your mind, your patience, and it gives you time outdoors to soak in vitamin D, oxygen, and who knows what else from the trees and plants. If you live in a city, investigate public park spaces. If you live in a rural area, investigate great places hidden away. Stay safe, take a buddy if you're going somewhere remote, or at the very least, let someone know where you're going. But get outside and enjoy nature. Notice the different smells, temperatures, sounds, and scenery. And it won't even feel like Exercise.

Pixie's Yumspiration
Chew-me Yogurt

Suggested Ingredients: Grass-fed, low sugar yogurt (I like plain best, however), **Cooked Quinoa, Sunflower Seeds, Dried Unsweetened Cranberries, Cinnamon, Nutmeg**

Preparation: Open up some yogurt. Add a bit of quinoa – enough to be in every bite, but not enough to make the yogurt dry. Add a few sunflower seeds and dried cranberries. Sprinkle some cinnamon and a touch of nutmeg over top. Stir all together. Eat.

Consumer Quote: (from an 45-year old man) "I didn't think I'd like to chew my yogurt, but it's actually really nice."

Chapter 6
-Home Cooking-

Learn to Cook Like
an Italian Grandmother

In my journey to health, one of the best tools I've had at my disposal is Cooking for myself. I've had to learn how, however. I didn't grow up in a home where my mother made delicious meal after delicious meal. She had a couple of things she made well, but overall the food was bland, overcooked, and often laced with exhaustion and/or resentment. She was over-extended all the time and it's a wonder she was able to Cook us all three meals a day, everyday, given all the responsibilities on her plate. And, because she had very limited time, it was easier for her to just do it all herself, rather than enlist the help of her whining children who had no skills to offer after the Battle to Begin ceased.

By the time I left college I had mastered a few Home-Cooked dishes, but nothing fancy and I mostly ate out or relied on university fare during my four years there. Once I moved to New York, however, I needed to eat more at home in order to stretch my meager pennies each month. In my first few years there I mastered a few chicken options, paired with rice or noodles n' sauce from a packet. It worked just fine, until I stopped making anything but the rice or noodles. Any side veg or protein was scrapped in the name of money, time, or desire.

At the time there were many, many food changes coming into play on the heels of living on my own and in a new city. One of the hugest turning points came shortly after I moved to Manhattan. I got cast at a summer theatre near Niagra Falls. I was in the ensemble, but I got to solo with a symphony orchestra in the middle of the contract. It was a great summer on every level – except for food.

The theatre housed us in the local university's dorms. While the rooms and bathrooms were nice and enjoyable to stay in for two months, the kitchen consisted of one microwave, one toaster oven, and one refrigerator – for thirty people. By the end of the second day, the food people put in the fridge had spoiled. It simply couldn't cool all we had shoved in there as a cast. My New York roommates were also there with me that summer, so we decided to scrap the whole kitchen idea, rent a clunker, and eat out at the only option in town: McDonald's.

For six weeks I ate McDonald's three times a day, every day. I was the original "Supersize Me." By the end of the summer I had gained forty pounds despite dancing all day, every day, and eating nothing except the three McMeals. Additionally, by the end, I wasn't even eating all three meals just out of being sick and tired of the same tastes day in, day out. When I went for my annual physical at the end of the summer I was told I had an "extremely enlarged" liver and I was asked about my alcoholism. While I drank socially, in no way was I an alcoholic at the age of 23, having only recently begun even imbibing at all.

As Morgan Spurlock so brilliantly depicted for us in "Supersize Me," though, my liver was in trouble due to ingesting only sugar, salt, and fat all summer long. And I wasn't even drinking the soda most days! I am proud to say that as of writing this paragraph, I have not eaten one bite of McDonald's products since August of 2006. It was my birthday gift to myself that year, and it's the gift that keeps on giving. At this point, even the fake chemical smells they pump out into the air make me sick to my stomach. My body knows the smells are chemical imposters and it is revolted by them. Real food smells, on the other hand, have healed me, enlivened me, and exhilarated me.

The first time I remember experiencing a kitchen that intoxicated me was on Christmas Eve, 1993. My dear friend Doug took me to his family's home for the holidays – where I entered a real Italian kitchen. Doug's family was only one generation "off the boat" and consequently many Italian traditions held very firm for mealtimes – especially holidays.

Walking into Doug's parents' house was magical. Smells of tomatoes, oregano, basil, honey, seafood, bread, and countless other delicacies came flooding to me with eager joy and desire that I would fully drink them in. And I did. I stood in that kitchen dumfounded and awestruck that such scents could be produced inside of someone's home – and by two identical pocket-sized grandmothers.

"Mama" was Doug's grandmother and Rose was her twin sister. They were in their eighties and buzzed around the kitchen with the speed and strength of twenty-year-olds in child-sized bodies. Mama and Rose were only about 4'8" and absolutely adorable. They both still possessed thick Italian affectations in their English and much preferred to speak to each other in their native Italian.

Consequently, anyone in the kitchen felt like an outsider, in the way, and like an intruder. Mama and Rose weren't unkind, just busy with preparing a multi-coursed feast for twenty-five people. They didn't have time to lead Cooking tutorials for those of us entering their magical laboratory for the first time. However, given their ages, many of the grandchildren had begun to enquire about recipes and "how to" make each of their favorite dishes. Somehow, the torch hadn't been passed over time and now the catch-up sprint went something like this:

Grandchild: Mama, how do you make strufoli?

Mama: You get some flour, you get some eggs, you put them together, get out of my kitchen.

Grandchild: But Mama, how much flour?

Mama: Depends on the number of eggs, now get out of my kitchen.

<u>Grandchild</u>: When then, how many eggs?

<u>Mama</u>: It depends on how much flour, NOW GET OUT OF MY KITCHEN OR WE'RE NEVER GOING TO EAT!

What I learned from watching Mama and Rose Cook, however, is that they never measured anything. They Cooked firstly by smell and sight and then by taste. I watched them sniff a pot and add an ingredient, stir and leave, without ever tasting a drop. To them tasting it meant you messed up along the way, I felt. If they followed their noses and eyes – and their hearts! – the meals would be delicious. And they were. Over the years I had the distinct pleasure to eat their masterfully produced cuisine several times. I am so grateful Doug shared his grandmother's Cooking with me. Her example ultimately made me the great Cook I am today.

When I first started Cooking to help me lose weight it was so difficult. I used recipe after recipe, only to often be disappointed with the final product and the amount of time it took to execute. Often during one of these kitchen forays I would have an instinct to add something that wasn't listed or to eliminate something that didn't seem to mesh with the rest of the smells. Over time I started to listen to my instincts more and use the recipes less and less and less. These days I don't follow them at all. I read them for inspiration and then I venture out on my own pathway.

And here's what I discovered: Mama and Rose sniffed first because the food led them to the answers. Depending upon how fresh something is, if it's organic, how it was preserved, etc. a food behaves, tastes, and Cooks differently. When I sniff my way through preparing my meals, they are always delicious. Next I make sure they are visually stunning and filled with as many of the colors of the rainbow as I can. Finally, I think of the Tastes of Life: Bitter, salty, sweet, pungent, astringent, and sour, and I try to include them all. Voila! A one-of-a-kind "recipe" occurs.

So, while I give you "recipes" at the end of each one of the chapters in this book – there aren't exact measurements for you to follow. I can't give them to you without meeting your food and sniffing it, feeling it, looking at it, and learning which flavors need to be the "star" of the dish. I'll give you a road map and the rest is up to your nose – it always knows. If the smell of the food doesn't excite and stimulate you during the preparation then it's not your star.

One final note about Mama and Rose: The thing I felt most in that kitchen was love. The room swirled with it, and therefore the food did too...and it made it taste amazing. When you Cook, infuse your food with love and gratitude and each recipe you share with others will elicit the comment, "What's in here? There's something I don't quite recognize, but it's incredible. What is in here exactly?" Don't try to recreate any of these recipes without love and gratitude thrown in. Those two ingredients will make your Cooking amazing every time.

...And eat more veg. Always more veg.

Pixie's Rx

Follow Your Nose – I search out food smells everywhere – spice markets, bakeries, pizza shops, etc. – and I allow them to inspire my next dish. The next time you are someplace that has REAL food Cooking (not fake smells from fast food places) . . . sniff, sniff, and drink it in. I have found that concentrated smelling also curbs my appetite. The smells fill me up!

Read For Inspiration – Whenever I don't know what to Cook I read recipes. Not to follow them, but to start my creative process. I flip through old cookbooks or Google different foods to see what recipes come up attached to it. After a few reads I am usually inspired toward something extremely delicious – and uniquely mine.

Include Spices "L," "V," and "G" – In addition to spices we eat, nothing flavors and enhances a dish like "Love," "Gratitude," and "Variety." Firstly, when I'm Cooking I make sure to think loving thoughts throughout. Even if I'm Cooking a quick something, I make sure the love is there first. If I'm Cooking for others, I actively love each of those who will be eating my creation as I add each physical ingredient. Next, there's gratitude. I thank each ingredient. If it had a personality, I thank it for its sacrifice for my benefit. If it's a plant, I picture what it looked like alive and I thank it for being such a beautiful contribution to my life. And finally, I make variety my main spice in Cooking. Challenge yourself to try new tastes, textures, and combinations. Enjoy that you have the ability to make your food as exciting – or bland – as you want, but mix it up! Have fun – and thank yourself for doing it!

TV Teachers – There are a variety of options from PBS to Networks to Cable. I began by learning from Julia Child on PBS. Many of the techniques she used were easily learned just from viewing. These days I enjoy Top Chef. I love seeing what chefs from all different backgrounds do with the same directive. Let the work of others inspire you in your own kitchen.

You-Tube U – Same idea as the TV, but you can find anything, practically, that you can imagine – often executed by someone just like you or me who just wants to share their expertise. I would also add iTunes to this list. There are tons of free classes on there on almost any topic you can think of.

Volunteer Sous Chef – Canvas friends and family to see who is an amazing Cook. After you've chosen someone, ask if you can come Cook with them sometime. Offer to do whatever tasks they need – such as chopping and/or washing dishes – and learn from them by watching. Ask them about their process and where they find their inspiration. I suggest doing this often and with several different people if possible. Regardless if it's one time or many, though, you will improve your skills immensely just by experiencing the smells and sights in real time.

Play Iron Chef – Sometimes when it's time for me to make a meal I simply don't feel like it, so I have to make a game of it for myself. One of my favorites games is "Iron Chef." I look in my refrigerator or cabinet to see what's there, pick an "ingredient of the day" and start Cooking – with commentary, of course. "Kwee-zan! What is she making?" Or I'll give myself a Bewitched Challenge a la, "Darren is bringing Mr. Tate over for dinner in an hour! Mr. Tate wants a Thanksgiving feast! How close can I get to it without magic?" Every time I use one of these techniques as motivation I end up having a ball - and making great food, too.

Martha Stewart Me – I like to challenge myself to present a plate that looks like the domestic diva herself designed it. I use the food as my sculpture medium, creating gorgeous options that "look too good to eat." Often I view myself as a "next generation" food artist, elevating Home Cooking to be viewed as "World's Most Exclusive Restaurant You Can't Get A Reservation For!" I think about the visual aspect from the beginning of the Cook, and I view it as an essential ingredient. And, I like to imitate Martha along the way.

Add In Game – I often don't have time to make a meal from scratch, but I want Home Cooked food and I'm tired of straight leftovers. So, I've learned to use my leftovers as a new meal starter. If I have a small amount of mac & cheese, I might add in some frozen veg and some tuna. Voila! A cheesy tuna casserole in minutes. Or if I have some cinnamon quinoa left over from breakfast I might add some curry, raisins, nuts and cauliflower to make an awesome savory lunch. Be creative and use all your leftovers up without feeling uninspired and unsatisfied. It saves time, too.

Start Simply – Master one dish at a time. Start with rice or quinoa. Keep making versions of it – as a side dish, as a main course, as a dessert. Don't make yourself sick of it, but master one dish and then move onto others. Find out what you like to Cook, and how you like to Cook. I love to Cook on a stovetop. I'm not fond of baking and grilling. I'm learning to use my oven better, so I'm liking that more. I'm a master with making greens, and I love that they come out perfectly every time. I also love making cold salads. My tuna fish is famous. I mastered it one summer. Pick your favorite simple dish, and enjoy the exploration of mastering it in your own kitchen.

Pixie's Yumspiration
Pottawaddagot

Suggested Ingredients: Since this dish is "A pot of what I've got", I can't suggest ingredients, per se. Look around your kitchen. Do you have a protein that needs to be eaten? How about some veg? How about something starchy? Can you imagine those flavors blending into something wonderful? Then put some water in a pot, throw in your items, add some herbs and spices, and make a one-of-a-kind meal out of "waddagot".

Preparation: Chop stuff, put it in a pot of water, bring to boil, then simmer for as long as it needs. Have fun with it! Then eat it.

Consumer Quote: (from a 72-year old woman after I whipped up a Potta in her kitchen) "I could have sworn there was nothing to eat in this house, but this is amazing and delicious!"

Chapter 7
-Education-

Planning For the Frost

Recently, I was in Uganda (I LOVE saying that, by the way – it makes me feel like I'm really living my life). While I was there I was struck by the lack of immediacy in the culture. While musing about it with one of my colleagues temporarily over there (a brilliant writer named James Magruder) he said, "It's because they don't experience frost."

Apparently there is a huge study going on of cultures that don't have frost, and how those cultures don't plan ahead, as a rule, because they haven't had to for survival. Food won't go away, unless there's a drought. There's no need to plan for fuel and warmth in colder weather because there is none. It's a different sensibility, but one I believe we are creating within our own society.

Currently, other than worrying about paying for it, we don't have to worry about food in our society. We produce more "food" each day then our society can – or should – eat. We have more than sufficient amounts of shelter, even if there are people without homes. Because of the advanced state of our culture, there are many ways in which we too don't plan for a frost.

On the flipside, I think of Vermont. This past summer I spent four days hanging out at Calvin Coolidge's estate. I was struck by just how much equipment and how many tools they needed to keep food plentiful throughout the year. So many gadgets to process apples that I didn't want to stand and count them all. Canning supplies, salting and curing tools, amongst other tools whose purpose is largely unknown and currently unnecessary.

I feel we are in the same boat with medicine. Homes used to contain herbal and holistic remedies used to mitigate illness gently and at home. We still have a version of this with over-the-counter meds, but if those go off the market or expire, then they are no longer useful. Also, those remedies are largely chemical and often harsher than necessary to soothe what is ouchy.

We are also this way about facts, phone numbers, addresses, maps, and a host of other things. With the advent of the Internet and search engines like Google, we no longer commit things to memory, storing them with great reverence and care – understanding that knowledge is power and also leads to autonomy in many ways.

I think one of the best things I continue to do for myself throughout this journey is to increase my level of Education on all fronts. These days I am hungry to learn about almost everything. I want to understand as much as I can about my Body, Mind, Spirit – as well as the universe that swirls around me.

Education is often seen as superfluous, something only for the young, or as some sort of elitist action. I don't believe any of those things. I believe the mind is hungry throughout our life and if we don't feed it, in its starving it will reach for whatever stimulation it can get – often leading to addiction and/or addictive behaviors. The mind needs to be fed. Not with chemicals and substances, but with knowledge, critical thinking, and the ability to make a plan – should a frost arrive.

As I look around the U.S., especially, I see we are in a deep frost only we aren't recognizing just how much is dying off under the sparkly, beautifully shimmering ice crystals. We are dazzled by the new experience, rather than understanding and accepting that it's better in the long run to keep vigilant and plan ahead. We need to stay focused on learning how to thrive in this new society, not relax into the ease of the whole thing.

So, how DOES one begin to prepare for the frost? By learning that it's coming, first of all, and then watching for the signs. And, as you're watching, readying for its arrival. And, what am I really calling frost in this instance? Well, that which kills off our vitality, our life . . . and for each one of us that is something different, and part of the Education is learning what is your frost.

Each one of us is completely, entirely, and utterly unique. My frost is not the same as someone else's, and my frost has also changed over time as I've learned to prepare for it – and therefore it can't rob me of my vitality and goes away. But what I've noticed is that frosts keep coming, and my preparation needs to, too.

Currently, my least favorite frost to deal with is weight regain. It's a very scary part of my picture because I know what I felt like – and how sick I was overall – when I carry excessive pounds. But, my body is ever changing, and therefore what I ate yesterday may not be what I need to eat today in order to remain the size I feel my best inhabiting.

My Education in this area has been, and will continually need to be, ongoing. What is "food", and what are "edible like-food substances", or "ELFS". What additives, such as colorings and preservatives, are causing my body to hold onto weight or are leading me to unrealistic hunger or emotional distress, such as depression. I've had to learn what is a marketer's ploy or a government's bowing to commerce or what certain buzzwords (like "all natural" – which basically means NOTHING) are really defining.

I've had to take myself back to school, and this time I actually want to master the subject, not just pass a test or an individual course. I want a PhD in MY BODY, so that when I feel the frost coming close, I can prepare, lose as little growth as possible, and flourish when the frost disappears again.

Each year I listen to my mother discuss the strawberry patch in her yard. She has to be vigilant, as spring is beginning, of those last bits of winter that may come to destroy the delicate flowers just peeking their petals out and promising fruit for later. I always marvel at her diligence in caring for those fragile blossoms, saving them from destruction and shepherding them through.

I want to be as diligent as my mother is with her berries with my fruits. I am a work in progress – always – along the way, but I keep at it now, the ever-dedicated student, understanding that Education is, and always has been, salvation for me. It saves me from the unknown, and gives me power and security and it has also given me my health back.

Weight regain is my frost, but so is sickness. Having spent the first thirty-six years of my life chronically ill, mostly out of self-care ignorance, I continue to learn what to look for, how to keep improving my intuition, and boosting my immunity daily. Will all of that keep me absolutely well? Maybe not. There are SO many other factors, such as environmental and accidents, that could come into play. However, by keeping myself learning I am also preparing to be equipped as best I can be, should that frost of sickness reappear.

Whatever your frost, Educate yourself to endure it, thrive in its departure and then learn in hindsight how to lose even less blossoms and fruit the next time. The Boy Scouts have been telling us for years, "Be Prepared" . . . and you can't prepare for what you don't know might be coming. What is Your Frost, and how will you cover yourself when it arrives? I hope, like my mother's strawberries, you – and I – will thrive and be able to welcome the thaw.

What is Your Frost? Have you prepared for its arrival? Oh, and eat more veg.

Pixie's Rx

Shhh . . . – I'll probably say it a few times, but for free learning get thee to your Public Library! Your tax dollars really pay for it, so you might as well take advantage of the fact it's there. Plus, it's a great reason to turn off your cell phone. Nobody likes to be shooshed – especially by a librarian.

"What Do You Do For A Living?" – One of the easiest, cheapest Educations I've had is in talking to people. People LOVE to talk about themselves so if you find someone with a profession that can help you with your quest for knowledge, ask away! In my experience, people are more than happy to share their expertise, within limits, of course. People still need to make a living!!! Don't ask for them to perform a service for you, but ask them to Educate you about their work. Plus, you might make a new friend.

Teducation – Ted Talks (ted.com) are my favorite new "free school." It is incredible just how diverse the topics are and what a wide breadth they encompass. Plus, with each talk under 25 minutes in length, they are a quick, concise, and extremely poignant resource.

Teacher Trade – What do you want to learn? What do you have to teach? Every one of us can teach something. Maybe you know how to bake and decorate fabulous birthday cakes. Maybe you can sew curtains or mend clothing. Identify your expertise and then seek out trading it with another "teacher". Years ago a friend came to me asking me to teach her to belt (a style of singing). She asked if she could trade yoga lessons for singing lessons. As I was then 100 pounds overweight and would never dared step foot into a yoga class at the time, I loved this trade. Thusly, we embarked upon "Yoga-Sing", a weekly ritual of trading an hour for an hour, skill for skill. And I got to spend extra time with my friend!

Volunteer Here, There, Everywhere! – With a small time investment you can learn immense amounts by volunteering. Want to learn to cook for large groups of people? Volunteer in a soup kitchen. Want to learn about organic farming? Volunteer to help out at a local organic farm. I'm sure they will be happy to have an extra set of hands! Want to learn to build or improve your house? Volunteer for Habitat For Humanity. Hands-on training can't be beat – especially when it's for free, and helps someone else out in the process.

Community-Sponsored Programs – Check your local area for offerings. I have seen free gardening, yoga, poetry, and a host of other things in communities across the world. See what your community is offering. Take part. Meet your neighbors and learn new skills to prepare and expand you for all that life has to offer.

Listen to Your Elders – Some of the best Education to come my way has been from the tongue of an elderly person. If you aren't fortunate enough to have a Grandparent or Aunt or Uncle to fulfill this post, why not visit people at your local nursing home or assisted living center? These buildings are chock full of Educators who are willing and able to take on new students.

Scout Out Scholarships – Just recently I decided to go back for my Master's Degree – but I don't have thousands of dollars lying around and I don't want to go into debt. When I went to undergrad I worked to get scholarships. I wondered if those still existed . . . and it turns out they do! I just received my first $5,000 award, and more will follow. Just keep researching, applying, and seeing yourself holding that diploma!

Grant Me A Better Way – Much like scholarships, but with different criteria to adhere to, grants are a great way to pay for Education of some sort. Go online and seek out Grants for

Individuals. Thousands of grants are available at any given time and can be yours for a bit of time, patience, and effort. I love looking through available grants. Just reading descriptions and criteria help me to expand my ideas even further.

Study Buddy- Do you know someone currently in school? Become a study buddy for them. When I was in college I was a study buddy for several pre-med student friends. My job was to quiz them off of their notes before tests. It was an awesome Education for me in classes I would never have had time to fit into my schedule. I got to learn a little bit about a lot of subjects, and I mostly learned where my interests truly lay – and where trails went cold. Plus I really helped out some friends.

Pixie's Yumspiration
Roasted Roots

Suggested Ingredients: Sweet Potatoes, Beets, Parsnips, Turnips, Red Potatoes, Carrots, Olive Oil, Cumin, Cinnamon, Nutmeg, Salt, Black Pepper, Cayenne Pepper, Thyme

Preparation: Wash root veg. Cut into ¼ inch thick slices. Preheat oven to 400 degrees. Get out a cookie sheet. Drizzle olive oil onto sheet. Take root slices and rub them on each side through the olive oil so each side is lightly coated. Lay slices in a single layer on the cookie sheet. Sprinkle desired spices over roots. Turn each piece over and sprinkle same spice mixture onto the other side. Place into oven. Set timer for 10 minutes. Check at that point to see how veg are coming by sticking a fork into them. When they start to become softened, turn each one over. Place back into oven and check every few minutes to see when they are golden brown and getting crispy on the edges. Remove from the oven and serve.

Consumer Quote: (from a 72-year old man) "I haven't eaten turnips since I was a kid. I don't remember liking them then, but they sure are delicious now."

Chapter 8
-Creativity-

The Cube Farm v. The Stage

One of the biggest gifts I've been given is that of a Creative mother. My mom is constantly Creating something out of nothing. As a child I watched her turn slices of Wonder Bread into delicate flower arrangements of miniature roses, violets, and daisies. Just by adding a little Elmer's glue and some food coloring, Wonder Bread became a great sculpting material.

Or, she'd begin with a ball of yarn and end with a gorgeous sweater or afghan or scarf. A piece of cloth became a dress or part of a quilt. Shredded zucchini she'd grown from a seed became delicious bread, hot and steaming from the oven. In her work as a teacher she'd concoct projects she could do with her students that they would enjoy, but that would still teach them something – all on a very small stipend.

Not only was I able to watch my mother Create, but she taught me how to do so for myself. I got to try my hand at Wonder Bread flowers and knitting and sewing. My mother is a teacher and she lovingly taught me whatever I wanted to learn. Mostly what she taught me, though, was to be Creative on my own.

I guess it shouldn't have come as a surprise to anyone when I chose a career in The Arts. I learned as a kid that Creating stuff is awesome fun, so why not find a way to get paid for it? And, I have . . . sort of. What I mean by that is that I've made HALF my living as a Creative person. I've made the other half working inside beige cubicles where I was asked to dress "less Creatively", Create less dialogue with people (in other words – shut up!), and to be as automated as humanly possible.

In some ways I used the Cube Farms as places to cleanse my palate in between shows. Also, being there motivated me to get the next gig on stage. I saw the older actors sitting there, their souls aching for stimulation and a challenge or two that needed a Creative solution. I saw their stuck-ness as a caution to be heeded by me – DON'T LET THIS BE YOU! I didn't want to watch my dreams – and my beautifully nurtured Creative spirit – to atrophy and wither. I saw the sadness that can come from such a path. I didn't want that.

Moments when I've Created something are truly the happiest memories I have. They are also the moments when I am my best self. My heart opens and as long as I can keep my inner critic silent, I'm peacefully just doing, making, crafting. I feel connected to everything pure and divine and my whole self works together as a well-oiled machine, producing incredible things from nothing.

When my vocation requires me to be Creative, I am a happy girl. I'm more energetic, I'm more productive, I'm much nicer to be around, and I feel "right". But more often than not these days I've been at the Cube Farm more than on a stage, or pursuing some other Creative pursuit. Because of a long list of factors – some of which I can't do anything about, like age – I don't have the same opportunities for Creative work right now. Which is sad because the Cube Farm bores me. To tears. Many, many tears.

But I can't sit around for my life crying and bored! In a way, having this extended period without the career I had come to enjoy on stage as my main financial support was the best frost a girl could ask for! It forced me to get Creative on my own – or risk heading full-on back into a life of sickness and ill health. I have lived the life of a working artist. I have also lived the life of a corporate cog. For me, there is NO comparison. So when my performing opportunities became less, my Creative mind woke up more.

65

This Creative awakening has produced incredible, unexpected results. I never imagined I would be a public speaker, but now it's one of my favorite new jobs. I never dreamt I would author a book, but now I'm finishing this one and I have several others mapped, planned, or begun. I never saw myself as a visual artist, but now I Create incredible things like giant room dividers from donated fabric, or beautiful boxes from paper, glue, and some trinkets.

Last year my husband was working as the Head Sound Engineer for the Broadway production of "A Trip to Bountiful", starring Cecile Tyson. Ms. Tyson was 89 years old at the time and definitely The Grande Dame of the building. Ed, as the Head Engineer, had to make sure her implements were delivered to her in a manner she would instantly know was "SOUND EQUIPMENT", but that could be hung outside her door – so as to not disturb her if she were resting or busy. In the past he'd used a simple bag from a high-end chocolate shop, but this time he wanted it to be a bit more special because it was Ms. Tyson.

Ed came home and commissioned a box of a certain size and a bag to contain it, both decorated especially for Ms. Tyson. And I had 48 hours – not a lot of time to make a great box – so I immediately got to work and was able to complete it on time.

That box and bag became the talk of backstage. Other people wanted a box of his/her own, and Ms. Tyson asked to "meet the artist". The director of the show, Michael Wilson, requested a moment with me. In the midst of nothing but Cube Farm in front of me for months, I was given an oasis when my husband commissioned that first box.

I made boxes for the others who asked, and presented them on opening night. I had such an amazing time making them! I was sad when I finished the last one, thinking it had been such a nice diversion from boredom. As an added bonus, Ms. Tyson commissioned a second box from me a few weeks later. As I presented it to her she hugged me and thanked me so warmly that it brought tears to my eyes. Just some glue, paper, trinkets, and a Creative mind allowed me an escape from boredom AND a personal performance of one of my favorite lines from any movie, ever: "The secret's in the sauce!"

That secret, for me, is Creativity. Nurture your own and see where it takes you. Oh, and eat more vegetables – in a Creative manner, of course!

Pixie's Rx

<u>Fairy Finds</u> – A Fairy Find can be anything from a coin found on the sidewalk to a piece of furniture you rescue from the curbside trash pile to a feather that blows across your path. At this point I have a whole closet full of awesome finds that await my Creative touch. Repurpose items, redecorate them, or just play with it! When a fun object finds its way to you, see where it leads your imagination. And, when you're done with it, let someone else "find" it if you'd like . . . then imagine where it goes and what becomes of it!

<u>Etsy Exploration</u> – If I ever feel stumped for ideas, I look online at Etsy.com - an awesome online marketplace for handcrafted items. Browsing around for even just a few minutes can inspire me to get busy on Creating something new. It reminds me just how Creative humans can be.

<u>As Seen In Nature</u> – Go outside into as much of a natural setting as you can find. Look around at the textures of the leaves, grasses, moss, bark, water, sand, or whatever is in front of you. I like to ask myself 'how have humans tried to recreate this?' For instance, moss reminds me of velvet. A shimmery pond reminds me of vinyl. Then I look for ways to make my own version of nature. How do I Create the look of water without having water? How do I give something the rough look of tree bark without it being rough? Look around and then see what you can Create that mimics what nature gives us as inspiration.

<u>Play With Yourself . . . Theatre Edition</u> – One of my favorite theatre games involves a bag of random items and the charge to incorporate them into an improvised scene, in zany ways. A hula-hoop becomes a giant hoop earring or the prototype for a new personal "force field protector shield". Many times when I'm feeling Creatively stuck I find that picking up a random object around me and going to the mirror for a little improv fun with myself can be a great tool. My favorite is when I crack myself up!

Rhyme Time With Inigo & Fezzik – In "The Princess Bride" is an awesome scene where the characters Inigo and Fezzik play a game where all conversation must be in rhyme. I have a few friends who will rhyme with me, but if they aren't around, I rhyme with myself – either internally or externally, doesn't really matter . . . just so long as my patter doesn't clatter! Enjoy the rhyming chatter. I'm off to make some cookie batter.

Mrs. Corry's Talking Shoppe – In the Broadway version of "Mary Poppins" my favorite scene was "Mrs. Corry's Shoppe". In the novel it is described as being inside the carpet and the drapes, consisting of people who have lost their language and need to buy new letters and words in order to communicate. At the audition I was asked to tell a story without words. I could use my body, face, and sounds, but no real words. I LOVED that exercise. Being in that show for most of three and a half years, I got really practiced communicating with my fellow cast members without words. Now I play "Mrs. Corry's Shoppe" in the mirror. Make up your own new language – and try to make it supercalifragilisticexpialidocious (I'm SO proud I can spell that without assistance!).

Squiggle Play – Make a series of squiggles either physically or in your mind's eye. Then morph the squiggles into other shapes – again either physically or mentally. See what you can see in each manifestation of the squiggles. Notice how your mind wants to organize them – or not. See if your squiggles stay stationary, or do you see them as figures in motion. See if the squiggles want names or if they have theme music that accompanies them. I like to make squiggles with shoelaces, pen and paper, spaghetti noodles, or just the markers in my mind. And most of my squiggles sing!

My Couch Is My Castle – As a kid one of my favorite Creative spaces was inside of the "couch castle" I made with the cushions and frame, along with some blankets and maybe a hula-hoop. Even today I still like to build forts and castles out of furniture and blankets. I take my favorite books, pens, paper, and a snack inside, and I escape to a magical land where anything is possible and I can Create whatever I want!

Recreate Me – I'm constantly striving to be the best me possible. Sometimes that means I need to "Recreate Me" from a LONG time ago, like before I was first bullied or before my heart was broken by someone I loved. It's easy to go only back to the person I became as a result of the event, but who was I before? I spend time with old pictures of myself and I try to reCreate the best of me. I'm also constantly looking for NEW ways to be, too, but I find Recreating Me is easier, often makes me feel younger than I am, and my best bits come shining through . . . just like they did before life boo-boos banged me up. Recreating Me not only gets my Creative juices flowing. It heals old hurts, too.

Parallel Universe Parade – I recently have become obsessed at the idea of all the universes interacting simultaneously with one another right here on earth. We humans have one, and right next to us live ticks, that have a wholly different universe. Humans and ticks may come into each other's universes, but it isn't a requirement of survival for either species. We live almost entirely parallel with many species. When I come into contact with another being now I try to imagine what its pure universe is like. What are the new dance fads amongst bees? What is the latest pick up scent this spring for stick bugs? What are the other praying mantises saying about Sylvia Mantis? She's eaten eighteen mates already this season! Put yourself in a parallel place. What's happening in that corner of the universe?

Pixie's Yumspiration
Mom's Carrot Cake

My mother, Linda Coffman, created this recipe in order to use up all the pulp she produced from juicing each morning. It's a brilliant way to use something normally thrown away – AND it's really delicious cake. Because this is a baked item, here is an exact recipe.

Ingredients:

3 Tbs. butter
3 Tbs. brown sugar
3 c. whole wheat flour
1 tsp. soda
1 tsp. salt
½ tsp. baking powder
2 tsp. cinnamon
1 tsp. stevia
2 c. pulp from juicer (use carrots, apples, beets
– no stringy vegetables)
2 eggs
2 c. milk
1 tsp. vinegar

Preparation: In a large bowl, cream butter and brown sugar together. In a small bowl, combine flour, soda, salt, baking powder, cinnamon, and stevia. Mix lightly with your hands. Add to creamed butter and sugar, again, mixing lightly with your hands. Add pulp and continue mixing lightly with your hands. In another bowl whisk eggs, milk, and vinegar. Pour liquid into flour mixture and stir with spoon until all flour is wet. Pour into ungreased baking pan and bake at 350 degrees for 30-32 minutes.

Consumer Quote: (from me) "Mom, this cake is AMAZING. And I can't believe it's left-over juicing pulp. Delicious."

Chapter 9

-Home Environment-

Party Supply #1: Bubble Wrap

I'm not the first to say it: Your Home is a reflection of how you feel about yourself inside. That's my variation anyway. And throughout many years I have found there to be a distinct correlation for myself. When my Home's a mess... I'm usually a mess in some capacity. Either I've over-committed myself and haven't left time to attend to my space, or I'm depressed and so I can't seem to function in a full enough capacity to keep on top of things. There are other options, but I know that if the house is "no bueno", Kate is "no bueno".

It took me a long time to realize the connection, however. For many years I would have been the roommate you dreaded! My stuff was scattered everywhere, and I rarely – if ever – felt the need to clean. Along they way many friends, roommates, romantic partners, and total strangers helped me to alter my ways and regard my Home as my sanctuary. Oddly enough, the total strangers taught me the most about how I wanted my Home to be.

I entered many strangers' Homes during my twenties for catering jobs. Essentially, I got paid to see how the "other half" lived. What I also learned was how to create my safe space, my sanctuary, my Home. As a cater-waiter I entered many awesome Homes. For private in-Home parties I came bearing food and party supplies, but what I really came with was my utter curiosity of how the wealthy people of New York City actually lived. I spent hours in each of those Homes, setting up buffets and serving guests, all the while observing my surroundings.

Many of the Homes were so ostentatious that they weren't comfortable. My favorite example of this was the

Home furnished entirely with pieces by Frank Lloyd Wright. The owner, a very uptight, high-strung man in his forties, wanted to show me – in great detail – his precious furnishings. And they *were* beautiful. The lines on the tables and chairs were infinitely pleasing to look at. The wood felt like butter under my fingers and I appreciated that the man suggested I feel the fine finish for myself. I imagined Frank, himself, lovingly sanding each beautiful surface. Of course now I realize he probably didn't do the sanding himself, but the image is still so vivid that I've decided he definitely sanded those particular pieces all by himself.

After the client showed me his incredible collection, he pointed to a role of bubble wrap and asked me to begin by covering the entire dining room table – including the legs – in protective bubble wrap. The table would be used as a buffet for the party, and the owner wasn't taking any chances that his beloved acquisition would be marred in any way. I understood – sort of. As the preparation for the party went along, however, I started feeling intensely happy that I didn't possess a household full of furniture that I was afraid would be somehow ruined, and therefore diminished in value.

Throughout our preparations I was asked to bubble wrap more than just the table. Arms on chairs, the back of a side table he didn't want to somehow "get shoved against the wall." By the time the guests arrived, very little of Frank Lloyd's creations were visible to the naked eye. Most of those stunning lines were hidden under the puffy and uneven bubble wrap. The food and beverages on the buffet all sat at slight angles, and many pitchers tipped and spilled as the night went along.

At the party's end, as I was freeing the furniture from its wrappings, I noticed how the host had disappeared. After I undid the last piece of bubble wrap, I went to look for him. The apartment was a sprawling place with large rooms, high ceilings and plenty of space. I didn't find the owner in any of these luscious spaces within the apartment, though. I finally found him sitting in front of the TV in a tiny, tiny, room at the back of the apartment, without any enjoyable view from the window.

The room wasn't even big enough for a full-sized couch. Instead he had a loveseat, with a small footstool in front and then a TV just a few inches away from the opposite edge of the footstool. The room was clean and uncluttered but really nothing much to regard. I noticed right away that the furniture couldn't possibly be by the famous Frank. I also noticed this was the first time I had seen the owner of the apartment look at peace in any way.

As he paid me for my work he stated, "Isn't it ironic that I spend all my time in what used to be the maid's quarters." He didn't say it as a question. It was a statement. Here he was in this giant apartment filled with priceless treasures, and his only comfortable domain was the maid's room. I agreed with him that it WAS ironic, as I immediately flashed back in my mind to my first NYC rental, which was the maid's room in a giant apartment on the Upper West Side. When I lived in the maid's quarters I couldn't wait to leave. I felt trapped by the small space. It felt like a cell. I also wanted to live better than a maid had.

As I left that catering job that night, I assessed my own Home. How much of it did I actually "live" in? How much was filled with things I "treasured", but weren't really all that useful? How could I challenge myself to really inhabit ALL of my Home – not just the places I habitually paid attention to?

Each time I had one of those catering experiences, I refined my vision of my PERFECT HOME ENVIRONMENT to match what I needed to be content, comfortable, functional, and proud of my creation. I stole ideas from many interior designers, I'm sure. I noticed what Homes felt full of love and positivity and which ones felt heavy and not at all "Homey". I noticed how the people were. If I were in a positive feeling Home, the owners were generous, kind, open, and welcoming of me. If I were in a non-Homey-Home, the owners treated me like "staff", never addressing me as a person, and never connecting with me in any personal way.

These days my Home is my Castle. My husband christened our Home "The Sky Castle" shortly after we bought it, and I have been the Queen of the Castle for many years now. I love what we have created there. I love that my Home is a living space where I can be creative and calm and content. I love the way that it speaks for me more clearly than any words I could choose would. I also love that – like me – my Home is an ongoing project in constant need of care, maintenance, and persistent attention to its ever-changing needs.

I've succeeded in making my Home my sanctuary. It's one of the most healing things I've ever given myself. To feel as if I utterly belong – and am in the right place for my well-being to continue – is awesome. What can you do to make your Home a true reflection of the "You" you want to be? How can you inhabit your Home better? How can you create your own sanctuary? I may not have a Home with Frank Lloyd Wright furniture, but I also don't have to bubble wrap before a party! Works for me. Oh, and in my Home we eat tons of veg. Try doing that in yours!

Pixie's Rx

The One Who Cleans It, Owns It – Whenever I want to feel more "at Home", I clean my house. Nothing is better than living in a clean Home – especially when I know how clean it is because I'm the one who cleaned it! When I was in Uganda I saw women "cleaning" the floors of their dirt huts with handmade brooms. While one could argue that sweeping away loose dirt doesn't make a dirt floor any less dirty, I saw the pride and ownership in these women's faces and I understood them. Cleaning is a beautiful way to really inhabit one's Home. Put on some great music and enjoy!

It's Time to Move! – I've noticed that those who move residences frequently tend to have less stuff, which makes total sense. Each time I've moved I end up shedding tons of unnecessary items from my life. Even though I haven't actually moved in years, I find it helpful to assess my possessions with a mover's eye. Would I take this to my next Home? No? Then it's not welcome to live here anymore either! Find charities to take useful items for a nice tax write-off. Or, sell really great stuff on Ebay and put the proceeds towards a remodeling project you'd like to do. Aim to leave a shelf or drawer empty – and feel "just moved in" all over again.

Maybe the Bookcase Should Go Here – I'm a big fan of moving furniture in my Home. Ever since I was a little girl I've rearranged my spaces with some frequency. It's a great way to move stuck energy in a room, and clean into tough-to-reach corners. Sometimes I end up putting things back where I first found them, but it always feels better no matter what.

Set A Sacred Space – Find a corner, a shelf, a wall, or maybe a whole room to become your "sacred space". My space is a beautiful oak shelf in our bedroom. On it I have a crystal star from Tiffany's that was given to me by Marvin Hamlisch and

Craig Carnelia after the pre-Broadway workshop of "Sweet Smell of Success". I surround that star with various ever-changing items like pictures, quotes, angel and fairy cards, or beautiful seashells. Those items on my shelf are to help me remember my purpose, ground my present moment, and pull all of my parts together as well as I can. Give yourself your own sacred space.

Calling All Color – I married a man who has an enormous love of color inside a Home. Such an idea hadn't fully been on my radar given that I'd lived in rental properties for years, which prohibited me to paint color on any walls. Now that I live within beautifully painted colored walls, I've come to realize how much color affects my overall wellness. When I travel a lot or work in a corporate setting for a while, I find I'm starved for interior color. In those instances I pull in color whenever I can. I use scarves as table runners, or I'll arrange books by their spine colors, attempting a rainbow effect. Find ways to bring more color into your Home Environment and see how your mind, body, and spirit respond.

Knickknack Show and Tell – At the age of forty-four I have realized the insidious nature of knickknacks. On vacation stops they call out "TAKE ME HOME WITH YOU!!!!" When relatives pass away boxes arrive with carefully wrapped treasures that used to give life and beauty to the deceased's Home. So now I have a rule: If it's not worthy of a SHOW AND TELL presentation, it doesn't live with me. A zebra from Uganda comes with the story of the open-air market where it was purchased and the life-changing events that occurred daily while I was working there. The Meneheune was made by my beloved Great Aunt Ines – who believed herself to be a gnome named Pepe. Each item needs a tale worthy of being told by me – or I don't need the item. Set unwanted knickknacks free! Sell 'em, give 'em, or donate 'em, but give yourself the gift of more space . . . and better stories.

Change With the Seasons – As the seasons change, change your décor – in whatever way you can. I still have far more knickknacks than space to present them in an uncluttered manner, so I rotate them with the seasons. It's fun to constantly see "new" items popping up, even though they are things I've already had. A friend's mom gave me some of her old table linens, so those alternate, too. Towels, sheets, decorative pillows, curtains, etc. can all be switched and usually they are items already inside your Home. If you live somewhere without seasons, make a quarterly schedule and do it anyway – and newly enjoy your old stuff year after year after year.

Let In Some Air, Please! – I can always tell when I enter a Home that never has its windows opened. The air inside feels stale, stuck, and dead. Before air-conditioning took hold, Homes were frequently aired out – even on cold, brisk days. When I clean I like to open every window in our Home and enjoy all the freshness that comes with exchange of air. Make time to air out your Home. If there are spaces without windows, use a fan or two, to help circulate the air around. As an added bonus I often find that dust bunnies are blown out of hiding and I can easily nab 'em!

Get Into Green – I'm the first to admit that I don't have a green thumb. But, I'm learning because having plants in a Home is just an awesome thing in my opinion. Having alive, growing things inside my Home helps me to feel vibrant and inspired to grow myself! Every time my African violet blooms I'm in awe. And, I've discovered there are plants for people like me who don't yet "speak plant". I have several different varieties that stay beautiful even when I over or under water them. They somehow adjust to my shoddy caretaking – and they remind me just how resilient growing things can be, including me. Ask around for cuttings from friends. I have found it quite easy to find plant enthusiasts who will gladly share their botanicals. As an added bonus I often think of who brought a certain plant into my life. Then I get two beautiful things to experience in that moment!

Set the Stage – I look at my Home Environment now as the most important stage I can set foot on. What does that stage tell an audience? What does the "set" look like? Does it reflect who I feel I am outside my Home? If not, what is off? What is the mood on stage? Is it tense and drama-filled or fun, warm, and inviting? Each morning when I rise, I set the stage for the day. I make my bed, open the curtains, light some soothing incense, put on a kettle of water to boil, put on soothing music, etc. I let my Home tell the story of how I want my day to go. As a child I woke up to chaos, loud speaking, and a frantic "we're late" energy. There weren't routines to set the stage so that a better story could be told. I find when I look to set the stage – whether that be the morning calm or an afternoon project that requires upbeat music and open windows or another scenario – my Home reflects my story in mood, smells, lighting, orderliness, etc. Set the stage so well that you'd welcome a visitor anytime, from anywhere. My Home always speaks for me. I prefer to be the director of the stage – not a visitor who doesn't belong there.

Pixie's Yumspiration
Comfy Tuna Casserole

Suggested Ingredients: Whole Wheat Noodles, (or if gluten intolerant, pick a noodle), **Tuna, Cream of Mushroom Soup, Olive Oil, Mushrooms, Onions, Zucchini, Carrots, Dill, Black Pepper, Cheddar Cheese, Potato Chips**

Preparation: Put on a pot of water to boil pasta noodles. Chop onions, zucchini, carrots, and mushrooms into small pieces. Preheat oven to 350 degrees. In a skillet on medium heat, sauté chopped veg until softened. Once pasta is boiled and drained, place it into a casserole dish. Mix into noodles the cream of mushroom soup, sautéed veg, dill, and black pepper. When well mixed, cover with cheddar cheese and a few crushed up potato chips. Bake until cheese is melted and casserole is bubbly around the edges.

Consumer Quote: (from an 48-year old woman) "This tastes like home – only better."

Chapter 10
-Relationships-

Together, I Stand; Divided, I Fall

This topic immediately causes my palms to sweat because I'm fairly horrible at Relationships. I have them, but I've lost tons of them due to my inability to nurture them and give them the time and attention they deserve from me. I'm still learning. . .

Mostly I've learned that while it's easier for me to be alone, or to only have a few close ties, ultimately that doesn't keep me vibrant, fulfilled and feeling loved. I need a pack, a posse. . . a family that includes friends and relatives alike. In order to have that, though, I've had to learn – often the hard way – that Relationships can only work if I present a loving, kind, patient, and open me. And I have to accept that as I've changed, the types of Relationships that once were "enough" for me may not be now.

My husband and I met doing the out-of-town tryout of "Sweet Smell of Success". I was immediately attracted to him and set out to chase him until he caught me. It worked and two years after our meeting I was fortunate enough to become his wife. In spite of my obesity, chronic illnesses, and continually diminishing health, Ed loved me, proposed to me, and embarked upon a life living beside me.

And then I changed drastically. And while I could hardly recognize myself, Ed recognized me even less. Post-weight loss I would often approach him at a meeting point on the streets of Manhattan only to see him look past me in non-recognition. As unsettling as it was for me to be receiving a stare of non-recognition from the man I said "I Do" to just four years earlier, it was incredibly difficult for *him* to not be able to pick me out in a crowd.

Not only was I physically different, the entirety of me was changing. I no longer knew how to communicate with those who "knew" me prior to the weight loss. I realized at some point that without my costume of fat on, I didn't know who I was. I had become whatever people needed me to be, rather than who I felt I was. With each social interaction I became more and more unable to relate to anyone. About anything.

Ultimately I first had to cultivate a Relationship with myself. Who am I, and whom does that woman want to surround herself with? Since I had no answer to either question I set out for resolution.

Having a Relationship with myself was hard. First of all, I'd come to not enjoy myself, my company, my thoughts. Inside my head was an endless barrage of negative comments and self-annihilation that continually diminished me and made me feel insignificant, small, and unworthy of loving connections.

Writing in my journal didn't help as I would simply transfer the yelling to the page, concreting it for years to come. I'd always be able to open that journal and see what a mess I'd become with my "honest critique" of Kate Chapman. But whose critique was it really? I went to the mirror to find out.

As I gazed into my own eyes I saw the pain of a neglected partner. I saw the damage done from years of berating and ultimately – personal neglect. As I looked into my own gaze I thought of the rice experiment I'd just read about somewhere.

According to the article, scientists decided to see if emotional energy had any effect on the decomposition of food. They made a single batch of rice and divided it into three parts. In the first container the scientists praised the rice, telling it how beautiful and nourishing it was. The second container contained rice that had been chastised, lambasted and told it was horrible. In the third container they simply said nothing to the rice and completely ignored it. With each of these containers the scientists waited and watched to see the rate of decomposition of the rice in each bowl. As I read the study I was amazed at the outcome.

The ignored rice began to deteriorate almost immediately, turning quickly to mold and decay. Following behind was the chastised rice, although it stayed fresh longer than expected. The third container of "loved" rice took much longer than the other two containers to spoil. The study essentially showed that any attention is better than none, but loving attention can prolong the life of an organism.

In the mirror my eyes became the ignored rice. How long had it been since I looked into them? When was the last time I had met their gaze and said something kind? In an instant I flashed to backstage of "Les Mis" on Broadway. Each show my cast mate, Joy, used to force me to the mirror during Act II before the entrance to the barricade scene. Joy would force me to look into my eyes and say, "I love you Kate". While I had gone through the motions to get Joy off my back, I never meant it.

As I saw my hollow sadness staring back I thought, 'What if I actually meant it? What if I actually found love for myself and found a way to express it to myself daily?' Around the same time I saw Suze Orman on Oprah. I remember her saying to Oprah, "I have a crush on myself!" Huh? What would *that* feel like?

In the mirror I made a pact with my baby blues: "I will learn to love you, say loving things to you, and allow you to be vibrant and unspoiled." I decided then and there to get crushing on myself. I was already in an arranged marriage with myself, and like Tevya in "Fiddler" I asked myself "Do you love me?" Immediately my inner-Golda spat back, "Do I *what*?"

So for all these years of maintaining my weight loss I've also been courting myself. Sometimes I'm a great date – kind, courteous, loving me despite my faults – as my husband had done when he proposed to me. Sometimes I'm a terrible girlfriend to myself – unkind, demeaning, berating. As I look at both versions of myself with myself I've also come to see that my outer Relationships are only as strong as my inner Relationship to ME.

Building a network of loving support takes time and patience. There may be people who go away. While that's painful and will require much grieving, try to thank those people for their past loving of you and learn to search for new connections that are able to see you today, in your ever-growing ability to be better in your Relationship with yourself, and ultimately others.

As a beneficial side effect, when I love myself more, I am able to easily move away from those people who may not know how much love and care this woman requires. Eighty percent of it has to come from me, I've discovered, but I've also learned not to squander the other twenty percent on just anyone.

How are your Relationships? How is your marriage to yourself? What can you do to help move yourself to a kinder, more connected existence? Oh, and eat more veg – you know your body wants you to!

Pixie's Rx

Go to the Mirror, Boy! – As the lyric goes in the musical "Tommy", get thee to the mirror and really meet your own gaze for no less than three to five minutes. Look lovingly toward yourself. How does THAT feel? Say "I LOVE YOU". Work to mean it. Make time each day to gaze into your gaze. Don't stop. Make this a life-long habit. You are married to your body – those eyes – until you die. Don't squander the opportunity to love yourself. It's the most important earthly Relationship you'll have.

Bloodline Redefine – By my mid-thirties my familial Relationships were in a state of serious neglect. If you are like I was, do yourself a favor and re-meet those family members you've lost connection with. You may not end up Besties with everyone, but your family is part of you – whether you like it or not. Look at your immediate and extended family. See what kind of connection you can find with each of them. Choose the "easiest" one first and reintroduce yourself to them. As I've been doing this I've found that I truly have an AMAZING family filled with incredible men, women, and children. I don't have the same level of intimacy with everyone, and that's ok. I have more love in my life – and that feels great. If some of your family members are kept as email friends, only – that's ok too. Take care of yourself during this journey, tell your story to those who have earned the right to hear it, and open yourself up to their stories.

Found: Common Ground – What are your interests? What are your personal issues? What would you like to learn? Each of these questions can help lead you to a broader, more well-rounded arsenal of Relationships. Check your local area for free groups, clubs, or support networks to join. Then strike up a conversation with someone who catches your attention. Since you are attending the same function, start by discussing common interests attached to that topic. Branch out from there and enjoy making a friend who is learning who you are today.

Find Me on Facebook! – When Facebook first appeared I was resistant to its usefulness. However, now it has reconnected me with people I knew but lost track of over the years. Childhood friends can be some of the best reconnections you can make for yourself. Reminiscing has been an indescribably healing portion of my recent life. When old friends share pictures or stories that I've forgotten, I see a better, fuller picture of how I grew to be "the me" of today. I've also been able to reignite some great parts of my personality that had been extinguished along the way. Seeing yourself through others' stories can be powerful medicine!

Agreement #2 Will Do – One of my favorite books along the way has been "The Four Agreements", and specifically Agreement Number Two: "Don't Take Anything Personally." This tool has been one of the most helpful things for strengthening my Relationships with others. Each of us says or does things that can inadvertently hurt someone else if they take it personally. As I continually practice this action I am able to be more loving and kind to those I love, understanding that they don't set out to hurt me. Maybe a criticism is simply a bad way to make a request of me. I try to hear the request and NOT the part that feels "personal". Open your heart, put aside your ego, and grow closer to those you love.

Listen Like It's A Movie You Can't Rewind – I've noticed a very odd human quirk regarding Active Listening. We LOVE to listen to stories, but we'd like to be semi-removed from the actuality OF it, and if we know it can be repeated, we may not listen much at all. However, if we as humans are engrossed in a movie or Broadway show, we will sit – sometimes for hours – listening intently. When I noticed how I wasn't actively listening when friends, coworkers, or family members were talking to me, I started to explore the idea of watching each personal interaction as if it were an event I'd purchased a ticket to attend. Just this small adjustment has improved every Relationship I have. And I've heard some FASCINATING tales!

Dear Me, I Love You - Whenever I'm feeling the veil of depression begin its descent upon me, I write a love letter to me. Depression keeps me from connecting with those I love – and most of all with myself. So, I find some paper or stationary I like, a fun pen, and I write kind, loving words to my BODY, my MIND, and my shrinking SPIRIT. I laud my personal ménage a trois on its poly-amorous lifestyle, and lavish on myself the words I long for my whole self to hear. Not only do I feel uplifted and giddy after sealing it with a kiss, I know I get to have another tête-à-tête with myself when I find the letter tucked away sometime later. I put the date on these letters and I love going back and reliving my growth of my Relationship with myself. Sometimes, though, I choose to burn them, keeping our deeply passionate Relationship a highly guarded secret. Whichever way, I write love letters to me – which helps me to write them to others, too.

Befriend Your Neighbor's "Best Friend" – Do you have a neighbor with an adorable pet? Why not get to know the cute little beast? As a kid I helped my neighbors out by loving their chickens and rabbits. I'd go to their house, talk to their critters, and talk to my neighbors, too. As time went on I took care of their creatures when they left town on trips. I loved the animals, and I also got close with my neighbors – so close that they began to take me on their trips, and they had someone else watch their animals. Today I have a neighbor who loves our dogs passionately. Through loving our little poopers she has become one of our best friends. Reaching out through an animal is one of the quickest ways to bond with another human. And you can have the joys of having an animal without the entire responsibility of owning it. Win-win!

Be Golden – The Golden Rule is all I really need to remember when I'm in an interaction with another person: DO UNTO OTHERS AS YOU WOULD HAVE THEM DO UNTO YOU. For me that simply means BE KIND. I just want to spend my life with kind people surrounding me. My latest and greatest practice right now is exercising my kindness response. I try to be kinder to myself, my dogs, bugs that cross my path (if they don't bite, aren't a roach, and weren't unlucky enough to succumb to a complete reflex response – they live!), and people who do things that reflexively I find irritating or abhorrent. I try "kind". And most times I am immediately ecstatic about the results. TRY KIND. And notice how just that one, Golden Rule can change your Relationships for the better!

Play Well With Others – For me, this encompasses so many things as I get older; Don't be the friend who always cancels, don't be the person whose needs usurp all others, and remember to ask about the other important people in the other person's life – to name a few. For a long time I'd stopped playing well with others . . . and so they stopped playing with me, at all. As adults we often have fewer and fewer close, intimate Relationships as the years go on. As people die, move, or simply grow apart, others aren't easily found to take their places. I'm keeping a close eye on this phenomenon in my own life, and reversing that trend. I don't want to end my life having only one or two close ties. I want a pack of people around me as I depart – so I need to play well now – while there's still so MUCH FUN to be had!

Pixie's Yumspiration
Twisted Grilled Cheese

Suggested Ingredients: Whole Wheat Cinnamon Raisin Bread, Jarlsberg, Gruyere, and Jack Cheeses, Butter, Pickled Jalapenos

Preparation: Butter one side on each of two pieces of bread. Slice one slice of each kind of cheese. Finely chop jalapenos. Heat skillet on medium high heat. When a drop of water sizzles in the pan, put the first slice of bread – butter side down – onto the pan. Place slices of cheese over bread and sprinkle with jalapeno bits. Cover with other slice of bread – butter side out. Turn the sandwich over after a short time – once side down has a light brown color to it. Just after turning sandwich, turn heat down to medium low. Smash pieces together with back of spatula. Keep turning and cooking until cheese is melting out the sides. Serve.

Consumer Quote: (from several who have partaken) "Damn that's good!"

Chapter 11
-Finances-

How Little Can I Do . . .?

One of my favorite jobs of my career was playing "Mrs. Claus" in The Radio City Christmas Spectacular, starring the Rockettes. From the very first moment I began, I felt "rich". First of all, it was the most money I'd ever been paid as an actress. Secondly I was wearing a $25,000 dress that was an incredible work of art. I LOVED that dress. I even loved it in spite of the fact that the designer seemed to charge by the pound – 25 pounds = $25,000. I felt like a magical gingerbread house when I was wearing it. I felt like I *was* "Mrs. Claus" inside that dress.

The third reason I loved that job was that I only worked for approximately twelve minutes per show. Now, sometimes we had four shows in one day, which made for a LONG day, but my actual "work time" was still only forty-eight minutes. Even though I had to be in the theatre all day, I spent my time reading, cross-stitching, napping, playing with my dog (who was "part of my contract"), or visiting with the awesome people I worked with. Basically I got paid to do all the things I liked to do each day anyway. And I was paid very well (by most people's standards). Even on a four-show day, I calculated I made $18.14 per minute! I realize that by the standards of, say, a corporate law firm, that that is "chump change" (my calculations = $21.25 per minute – for 8 hours per day, or more for a partner at a giant firm), but by most "normal people's" views, I was on Easy Street.

That was a job I held for five Christmas seasons. It got me out of debt, made each of those years a "Financial success", and allowed me to live in New York City and enjoy some of the unique perks my great city has to offer to those with Financial means. Radio City was also the job that brought me the mantra, "HOW LITTLE can I do for HOW MUCH money?" As those were some of the happiest days of my career, I've carried that sensibility into my daily life.

I'd love to say that since that day I've managed to make over $18.00 per minute every minute I work, but that's not been the case. I still live like most Americans of today who watch every dollar in their bank account. It's a difficult world out there for most of us Financially. But I don't believe it has to be so hard. I have found for myself that most of Finance is a mindset. While my first Money Mantra is "How little can I do for how much money?", my second – and equally important – Money Mantra is, "Money is the most replaceable thing we've got."

I often go to the Metropolitan Museum of Art in New York for an hour or two in order to enjoy some art. One of the first exhibits I often walk through contains thousands of coins from Ancient Egypt. Each coin is, indeed, a work of art. They were individually cast and made, usually of bronze or gold or another precious metal. Each one looks very similarly to another while still showing the discrepancies caused by human makers. I love them because they remind me that once those items were money, and now they are considered art, and therefore unable to be used for currency.

Even in my own life I am surrounded by money that has become something else when it was replaced by a newer version or a change in environment. I have books of antique coins that can't be spent in a store, but were once counted and regarded with the same energy I often give my currency today. Or I look at the bowls filled with foreign coins and notes that became useless as currency once I returned to the U.S. I have more Ugandan money in my hallway bowl than some Ugandans there make all year. To me, it's a cheap souvenir. To them, it's what they are chasing after every day.

Which is why the second mantra is SO vitally important. Money is a man-made, earth-bound distraction of gargantuan proportions. I know! As an artist for my entire working life I have not been "rolling in it" very often, and certainly not for very long (yet!). I've cried about Finances on a very deeply devastated level MANY times. I've mourned my career choices in the name of money. I've struggled right alongside of those who aren't sure where the next paycheck will come, or how much it will be when it does.

And, as of the writing of this chapter, the paychecks keep coming. Although I long to have the HOLY GRAIL of "You are a Financial Success" showing in six-months cushion in my bank account, I'm proud of where I am and what I've achieved by following my Money Mantras. I've been able to keep my Financial life fairly well in perspective. Yes, it's vitally important for life on earth – and yet, it's the most easily renewable resource man has created.

When I'm really, VERY honest with myself about the Financial health of my life, I can see how it has mirrored my health in other areas of my life. When I'm treating my life as a precious commodity that needs to be honored for its finite richness, I look at my bank account and there magically seems to be money there. I know it's because I'm too busy LIVING to stop its flow into my life. However, if I'm struggling to engage in my own plot line, I seldom can find two pennies to rub together.

Which brings me to my third – and final – Money Mantra; "If I find myself with no money, ask myself, 'How am I not doing my job of living well? How am I not showing up for the work of living?'" I believe with all my heart that there are enough resources on this planet for us all to live awesome lives. In order to access those resources, however, we need to do our part fully to earn those riches. That may mean something grand and splashy, or it may be something tiny and intricate, but it is for us to do.

My Radio City experience is one that keeps on paying me, even though I no longer work them. Over the five seasons as "The Mrs.", I worked with some incredible Little People. LPs, as they're called, are hired to play elves and other costume characters. Since I had a lot of off-stage time, and they were my elves, I really got to know most of the LPs I shared a stage with. And I *loved* them. They were some of the most fun people I've ever had the pleasure of spending time with.

Apparently America thinks so too, as most of them have been popping up all over TV during the past few years. There's Shorty Rossi, Sebastian and Ronald who all hung out on Pit Boss, and then I can turn to Little Women: LA and enjoy spending time with my girls Terre and Tonya, and – my favorite – Terre's boyfriend, Joe. All these awesomely talented people taught me about showing up, seeing opportunities, and achieving one's dreams. And they still do, each and every time I turn on the TV and catch one of them doing their thing.

The LPs showed me how easy I have it in life. Employers aren't afraid to hire me. As an actress there are far more roles for me than for any of them. I haven't had to have surgery after surgery after surgery all my life, although I do feel my medical history made us kindred spirits in some ways. We all knew what it was like to be poked and prodded and often disregarded as people.

They are disregarded as people more places than in an examining room, however. Random strangers treat them as freak shows, pets, children, or a number of other demeaning things. And yet I watched them show up for life, day after day, with kindness, humor, and a creative solution for making the next paycheck arrive. I watched them show up each day to bring others holiday cheer, and now they bring me wonderful memories and great fun each time I watch them show up on my TV screen.

Sometimes I forget to show up, though, and start to coast along through my days. I find I can usually get away with it for a while, but eventually my world starts to show I'm not doing my part. Because I've structured my life to put my inner comforts ahead of my outer comforts, my disengagement usually shows itself in my Financial health first. And that's when I know it's time to wake up, get to work, and start over with Money Mantra #1 in direct focus.

As with all items of self-care, it takes time, patience, and willingness to practice, practice, practice. Because money used to scare me and because I find numbers cold and boring when tethered to dollar signs, I keep my practice short and sweet:

Money Mantra #1 – How LITTLE can I do for HOW MUCH money?

Mantra #2 – Money is the most replaceable thing we've got.

Mantra #3 – How am I not showing up for work?

Mantra #4 – Eat more vegetables.

Pixie's Rx

Practice Away . . . With Pay – What is a skill you have – or you WANT to acquire – that could earn you income? When I was a small girl I learned to do basic sewing on a machine and by hand. As an adult I find it calming to sew. One of my first jobs in NYC was sewing for a costume shop. I didn't really know very much going in, but I learned quite a lot while I was there. Recently I've found a new way to turn my time sewing into a moneymaking venture. I'm still just a basic novice, but I'm using my limited skills to provide things to people with even less skills in that area, but who need some items sewn and are willing to pay me! In college I took a job in a church choir to practice my novice sight-singing skills and be paid. That turned into income in recording studios once I moved to NYC, because I sight-read so well. In the corporate world I got paid to type and use software programs at a high level. I now use both those skills for other moneymaking ventures. Find an interest, get good enough to be useful at it, and find someone to pay you as you practice away.

Trade-E-Oh! – As a child one of my favorite radio programs was "Tradio". People would call in and say "I have a child's bed that I'd like to trade for a wheelbarrow" – or something equally as bizarre. But as the show progressed, people would call, offer trades, and in the end most people ended up with what they needed – for free. There was also an experiment done where a paperclip was traded into a house. Especially in the U.S. I believe we have enough resources to go around. Be inventive and trade your way to a better Financial picture. You already traded our valuable time for the money you used to buy whatever item you no longer need. Don't lose your initial investment by throwing things away. TRADE THEM – and make your expired time generate new revenue!

Lock Up the Lincolns – A friend of mine mentioned he wasn't going to spend his $5.00 bills for the entire year. Each time he got a $5.00 bill in change, he simply put it into a box to use for a vacation later. I tried it for a month and found I'd amassed $60 without noticing. So, now I'm on a quest. Sorry Abe, but you're in LOCK UP for the next five years. I'm not sure how much I'll get, but I'm certain it will feel like the world's biggest windfall. It already does each time I see the stack in the box grow.

"Each Week I Am Worth More" – For the past two years I have noticed on Facebook that there is a New Year's idea for how to have $1378.00 in your pocket without pain at the end of the year. Each week of the year you put away the equivalent dollar amount; first week - $1.00, second week - $2.00, fifty-second week - $52.00, which equals $1378.00 at year's end. I love this clever, easy way to save some cash. I have added my own addition to the exercise. With each week and "deposit" I state "This week I am worth more than last week. Next week I will be worth even more." And don't be sad when the year turns over! You're not now worth *less* suddenly – you are worth $1.00 PLUS $1378!

"I Am Change" – About six years ago I started to notice change on the ground as I walked around NYC. I'm sure it's always been there, but it wasn't until I had changed from being an obese woman to being a thin woman that I noticed. I started looking at the ground as I walked in order to ignore the ogling of men, which had arrived along with my weight loss. And what I found was MONEY! FREE MONEY! I started picking it up and putting it aside. Each year I now get between $100 and $130 just for ignoring rude oglers! And each time I am fortunate to find some, I state a mantra, smile that I'm suddenly wealthier, and put the money in my pocket or purse. I even have a secondary saying for when coins are tails! Make it fun for yourself. Money is everywhere. You just might have to bend over to pick it up.

Out of Town Price – Many years ago as a young actress I realized that while having an acting job was great in many ways, it wasn't great if I went broke while doing it. Many regional theatres pay a wage commensurate with the cost of living for the area where the theatre exists. I live in NYC! While it's AWESOME that someone can live well on $312.00 per week in Mississippi, that is not *my* world. I found I needed to set an OUT OF TOWN PRICE in order to meet my financial needs in the BIG CITY. I was nervous at first, but I quickly learned that when I set a clear goal, the paychecks followed. When I set a price for myself based around real, attainable circumstances, I find the money follows. Set your price – and get it!

A Lot Here, A Little There – Many artists, myself included, work to Master the Art of Income Here + Income There = Enough All Around. The American mainstream dream of working for a company for thirty-five years, retiring with a great package, and living comfortably ever after is largely gone. While that causes unease amongst people who have never experienced other ways of earning, I'm not so sure it's a bad thing. Living in a land where multiple streams of income have always been my story, I've come to realize that once you get the hang of it, it's a very nice way of life. I never have to worry about all my income drying up at once. I don't have to work with the same people all the time. I don't have to work in the same environment all the time. And, I can stop doing a job if I really hate it. I can replace it with something else, if I plan correctly. Notice where you can make money in different places…and see how it equals enough.

Let 'Em Live! – My best financial advice ever? Stop eating meat. Eating a diet full of plants can keep more money in your bank account than almost any other action. Meat is expensive. Not as expensive as it really *should* be in my opinion, however. After all, it was a living creature. And while I'm not a vegetarian, I eat very little meat and I regard it with a lot of respect when I do by only buying humanely raised animals. And that one action has saved me thousands of dollars. If you need help to see animals in a different light, go to a farm. Spend some time with them. See them for the vibrant lives that they are. And more meals than not, choose to let 'em live another day. Oh, and watch videos of cows playing on YouTube. They look like dogs. Do you eat dog? Pigs and chickens are pretty cute, too.

Potta Wadda – This is my culinary specialty. The formal name is "Pot of What I've Got." This is a one-pot soup, stew, casserole, gumbo, etc. made solely with ingredients on-hand in a kitchen. Anything can become a Potta Wadda. On my honeymoon I made a fresh seafood Potta Wadda that my husband and I still reminisce about. This week I made a mushroom-based Potta Wadda that received my father's eager approval of, "Hey, that's pretty good!" He usually accepts a meal and gives a nod and "It was fine." He's not one to be effusive about food. Have fun playing and creating one-of-a-kind dishes, which will become memorable meals of all time, out of what's already sitting in your kitchen waiting to be used.

401-Kate Plan – I realize before I write this tool that it's going to cause some arguments. The crux of it is that I believe a dollar is never worth more than it is today. By tomorrow it has depreciated. Because of that belief, I don't believe long-term investments are necessarily the End All, Be All in Financial life. I feel the real answer lies in educating yourself about every option for Financial health that is recommended, and then make your own plan. For years I strove to put as much money as I could into my 401k plan. Then I watched it plummet just a few years later. I then listened to expert assurances that it would "come back". Well, it has, but it took several years and those dollars are now worth less than the ones I originally deposited in there. While it may have "come back", it certainly didn't return to me with any new friends.

Because of my money's temporary hiatus from my account that plan now seems not for me. That and other reasons are why I've looked around for different plans to emulate. I have known stories of people saving millions in their mattresses on a janitor's salary. I've also lost friends in their primes who where "all set" for retirement – and never got there. Make a Financial plan that fits who you are – and think outside of other people's boxes.

Pixie's Yumspiration
Red Beans and Rice

Suggested Ingredients: Red Kidney Beans, Water, Onion, Garlic, Bacon, Pork Sausage Links, Salt, Black Pepper, White Rice, Tabasco Sauce

Preparation: For best result – if using dried beans – soak beans in water overnight. Drain and rinse the next morning. For preparation of the dish: Chop onions and garlic into medium-small pieces. Chop bacon into ¼ inch pieces. In a skillet, sauté them until onions are slightly translucent. In a large pot, put enough water to cover beans by an extra inch. Bring pot to boil. Add onions, garlic, and bacon mixture. Reduce heat to medium and cover pot. Brown sausages. Throw them into pot with beans. Cover and allow it to cook until beans are tender and a bit of a gravy-like sauce forms. Add salt and pepper. Recover and let simmer while rice is cooking. Once rice is cooked, serve together in a bowl and sprinkle Tabasco Sauce on top. I even love them better the second day.

Consumer Quote: (from an 10-year old boy) "Is there more?"

Chapter 12
-Joy-

"No Worries": Adopting the Aussie Way

I am currently sitting in Sydney Australia. I am here to finally finish this book I've been hacking my way toward for five years. I came to attend a conference, but really to have a place with as few distractions as possible in order for me to work. How perfect it is to be here, in the land of "no worries."

Now, I'm not suggesting that Aussies have no worries, but their response to any request, question, or need is always punctuated by the phrase "no worries", which makes me smile and brings me Joy. I immediately am launched into a fantasy of a life with "no worries". What would that even look like? How can I punctuate everything in my life with that sentiment? Well, by responding to every request that life asks of me with my response to the Aussies this week: Smiles . . . but most of all – Joy!

When I am in Joy, I truly have no worries. I only have light, happiness, and ebullience. When I am Joyful I feel buoyant, uplifted, and ready to tackle anything. I smile, I laugh, and people want to be around me. Also, when I feel Joy I am full, expansive, and floaty. I am me – as my best self.

How can I stay in Joy, though, when at every turn there is something ready to strip me of it? For me, it has to remain at the top of my "to do" list. I have to remember I *need* Joy in order to feed my soul – so I don't end up overfeeding my body in the name of Joy. It can be confusing, though, because one of the things that bring me Joy is great food! However, when I have too much food, I rarely feel Joyful afterwards.

One of my favorite Joy-inducing activities is to think of things that might bring me Joy. What would give me no worries? What makes me squeal with the delight of a young child? Each day, as I find things, I make a mental note, add it to my arsenal of tools, and revel in its arrival in my life.

I also like to make up what the word would stand for if it were an acronym, instead of an actual word. J-O-Y = Just Open Yourself; Jump Often Youngster!; Jam On Yourself; Jinx Only Yuckiness, and other silliness such as that. I want to inhabit the word as much as possible, so I give it quite a bit of my attention. I'm diligent about it now because for so many years I simply couldn't find it. Joy was lost from neglect and underuse.

I've learned – the hard way – that when I can't see Joy, it has an impossible time finding me. For many years I had friends and family feeling my Joy for me. I looked to others to see how I should feel about something. Should I be happy? Is this what that feels like? Or, if I did feel Joy but someone told me not to, I would immediately shun it and inhabit the emotion I was told to have.

In many ways, I feel this is how and why I became an actress. Because I never knew HOW to feel about anything, I entered into a world where "how" and "what" I felt was defined by a character, a director, or other actors in a scene. I didn't have to make many decisions, and even if I made the "wrong" decision I could be guided to the "right" feeling by someone outside of me, like a director. Over time, however, I came to realize that the one emotion I couldn't fully "act" was Joy. Either I felt it, or I didn't. I couldn't manufacture it. I had to seek it out or allow it to enter my space if it arrived on my doorstep unannounced.

For me, Joy comes from within. From that place of purity inside of me that has been untouched by the outside. It is my essence, my innate core, and the place where life – and LIVING – are born. And being that it resides so far inside of me, I am the only one who can truly cultivate it, feed it, and make sure it isn't squelched and dampened.

So as I sit here in Sydney, finishing this book that is so important to me, I am reveling in my Joy – deep, unbridled, self-nourished, and fervently protected Joy. It's the most amazing feeling to be tapped into it so fully. I would love to say that I inhabit this space always. That would be untrue, but each time I am swimming in Joy – like now – I am able to carry a bit of it with me into the tough moment and remember "no worries" is a great place to be. And for me, that place is called Joy.

And eating lots of veg is also Joy-inducing – so eat some!

Pixie's Rx

The Pollyanna Effect – One of my favorite movies/books is "Pollyanna". I love her "Glad Game". In the Disney film I always remember Haley Mills, as "Pollyanna", explaining how it's played. I really think she explains it best, so watch the movie, but essentially the idea is that in every situation there is *always* something to be glad about; even something as sad as the recent death of my beloved father. I can be glad that I got to spend so much quality time with him in the last days of his life. I can be glad that I reconnected with cousins and uncles and aunts in a meaningful way. I can also be glad that I have one more angel watching over me. And I can be glad that each time I succeed in the game, I feel Joy.

Smile – Though Your Heart Is Breaking – At my lowest, loneliest point in life I read an article about the positive effects of smiling – even when it's not attached to a positive emotion. According to the article a study was done showing that smiling – even without cause – increases positive production of endorphins, natural painkillers, and serotonin. So, I tried it. So far I have found it works. I feel better, my mood lightens, and my frown lines have decreased significantly. Another study I read later involved actors. They studied those actors who were portraying dark characters and stories and found that as emotions were "acted", their body produced an equivalent hormonal response. From my experience as a professional actress for over twenty-five years, I would say that rings true. So, conversely, act happy . . . and your body will start to *feel* happy – and that includes your mind. So smile. And then smile some more – until it comes naturally on its own – bringing Joy alongside.

Baby Yourself – And by that I mean study to *become* one! Get in front of a calm, needs met, baby. They laugh constantly. At everything. When I'm around babies I try to find funny what I imagine they are laughing at, and I join them in their mirth. I have found it totally sends me around the bend to Joyville. This world, Earth, is hilarious in many ways. Become the baby you once were to reconnect to that place of wonder, hilarity, and Joy – and then inhabit it often.

Skip A Step or Two – Skipping is awesome! First of all, it's next to impossible to skip without smiling. Skipping and smiling are physiologically linked in my opinion and experience. Skipping also brings smiles to those who see me doing it. I don't worry about the thought behind the smile. I just enjoy that my skips have solicited smiles. As an added bonus, skipping raises your heart rate and is excellent cardiovascular exercise. Additionally if you can find a "Skipping Sibling" your Joy will be multiplied by theirs. Usually my Skipping Siblings and I end up in fits of laughter. What could be better?

Find the Funny – All of us have a sense of humor. Some of us have cultivated that part of us to be large and in charge. At this point, when I am looking to find Joy, I look around and find what's funny. Just a few minutes ago, for example, I thought I heard the manager of the restaurant in Sydney (where I am writing) say to a deliveryman, "Now you're sounding like an American!" I immediately looked up and they caught my gaze and apologized. I enquired "What exactly did he do that was 'American'?" "Not *American*. I said he was sounding like a *Married Woman!*" To which I quipped, "Oh! I can only imagine what you said – being a married woman myself." All of us burst out laughing and shared a great moment together because we chose to Find the Funny.

Merry Memory Markers – What is your favorite memory? Why not mark a reminder in your calendar to pause and relive that experience at least once a year. Or once a month. Or once a day. Studies show that lingering on happy memories leads to the production of inner Joy. Relive the good parts! Mark it down on your TO DO list so you remember! MMM...Merry Memory Markers Rock! So does reliving those great times.

Now, Baby. Now! – One of the biggest Joy producers I have found is to live presently. How many times do we simply go through the motions of life while dwelling on the past or the future? As often as you can remember, Live In The Now!!! Enjoy your present and give your mind a chance to be in THE NOW. Studies are showing a shift in brain activity from the right frontal area of the brain (where anxiety, depression, and worry live) to the left – where happiness, excitement, Joy and alertness hang out. Hang with the Happy Ones in the Now!

Attitude of Gratitude – All day I look around for things to say "Thank You" about. Thank you for the air. Thank you for that cute dog I just passed on the street. Thank you for the color blue. I'm not even directing "Thank You" to anyone or anything. I'm simply putting it out there. "THANK YOU!" is pure Joy – every time.

Stop and Smell the Roses – Smells can always transport us to a memory. Pleasant memories attached to certain scents can be accessed any time you want. Make a list of favorite memories. Remember the smells that were there, then find time to either sniff a real smell, or simply remembering the scent can even do the trick! Also, studies are showing that flower scents have a positive influence on your emotions. So, sniff those posies and enJoy!

That's My Song! – What's your personal Joy Anthem? Mine is "It's Gonna Be" by Norah Jones. From the first moment I heard that song it made me dance. Every time I hear it I associate it with several amazing personal memories and my mood soars even higher. Find your anthem and play it or sing it a capella any time you need a pick-me-up. Music is pure magic. Find your own Joy Anthem – and let it ring!

Pixie's Yumspiration
Summery Rainbow Salad

Suggested Ingredients: Baby Kale, Mixed Lettuces, Frisee, Radish, Carrot, Tomato, Sweet Yellow Pepper, Fresh Blueberries, Feta Cheese, Sunflower Seeds, Black Pepper, Olive Oil, Balsamic Vinegar

Preparation: Chop all veg into bite-sized pieces. Put onto a plate. Add some blueberries. Sprinkle over some feta cheese, sunflower seeds, olive oil, and balsamic. Top with some black pepper. Enjoy.

Consumer Quote: (from an 46-year old woman) "I wasn't convinced about your combination – especially the blueberries. But, I have to say, I'll make it for myself again."

Chapter 13
-Social Life-

The Sickly Petal

Of all the petals on my daisy, this one is the most withered and in danger of falling off. I LOVE the idea of a healthy Social Life, but the truth is I don't have one. In fact, I've never had one. I've tried various ideas of what I perceive it is supposed to be, but they haven't been all that sustainable. I don't mean to make it sound like I don't have friends, although I have many fewer of those than I'd like. Of the friends I do have, however, I don't have a healthy Social Life with them.

At this juncture my Social Life consists of a few events here and there, usually planned by someone else, and I generally struggle to make myself attend. I didn't gain good Social skills as a child. I rarely received "plays wells with others" checked as satisfactory on my report card at school. I wasn't raised in a way that nurtured that part of me. And since I'm outwardly friendly and open to new people, I am generally mistaken for someone with a great Social existence. But it isn't true.

The whole truth is: I'm STILL learning how to behave in Social settings in a way that leads people to wanting me to come back. My skills up until recently have been quite underdeveloped and I often said or did things that a woman of may age and desires in life wouldn't want to do. I often called negative attention to myself – because I didn't know how to be noticed in any other positive way, except for singing.

The truth is I'm an awkward nerd. I'm the girl who retracted into my imagination when I couldn't or didn't have Social outlets that were pleasing to me. I wasn't withdrawn. I just didn't speak "the language" well and so I was often very far behind in the conversations. Even today I read some of my friend's Twitter accounts and I have zero idea what they're talking about. People tell me I should Tweet – and all I can do is start to panic that I'll be trapped living my life in Haiku if I start.

Even Facebook is a difficult place for me to play. It brings out all my childhood feelings of inadequacy and isolation when I didn't speak the language of my peers. I find I'm happier being a reader and a liker rather than a constant poster. I find myself tenderhearted when a post I really loved doesn't get "liked" enough. And the whole statistical aspect of it feels like I've placed myself on some sort of popularity graph.

But I know – and studies have shown – that a healthy Social Life is often a determining factor of a long, healthy life – and I want that! I want to be surrounded by people of all ages for the entirety of my life. I want friends of all generations around me, sharing my time here on earth with me. And I don't just want work colleagues who might be sad that I'm gone, but aren't more closely tied to me than that. I want a community, a network, a Social fabric. But how's a Socially awkward girl supposed to get that during midlife?

I keep thinking back to my first landlord in New York – a ninety-two-year-old Russian Jew who had survived the Holocaust and thrived for many decades afterward. I was introduced to her by a college professor of mine. She had a room to rent that was perfect for my needs. I inhabited the former maid's quarters in Anne's very large Upper West Side pre-war apartment overlooking Riverside Park and the Hudson River. My shoebox of a room also had a thimble-sized private bathroom. In the living room was a Steinway that Anne had tuned weekly. She often encouraged me to use it as much as I wanted. It was a beautiful instrument.

The first week I lived at Anne's I realized she was no typical nonagenarian. Her Social calendar completely humiliated mine, and she often arrived home from an evening out well after two in the morning. Sometimes she attended the opera on the arm of a handsome young man. She went to museum galas with middle-aged socialites, often staying until the end of the party. She threw concerts in her home for charity, charging $10,000 per seat – and selling out the room's thirty-five chairs every time.

Anne's Social calendar was filled with visits from family and friends in addition to her special outings. I'd often come home to find the living room filled with grand nieces and cousins' children. Anne didn't have any children of her own, but you'd never have known that by the way she was cherished by each of the relatives who passed through her door. And every time I'd enter the happy gathering, Anne would invite me to join them. I did once or twice and felt honored to be amongst such love. And also uncomfortable. I didn't know my place in such a setting.

I only lived with Anne for about nine months. By that time I wanted to live with friends my own age. The impact those months had on me was deep, though. I can still see Anne, sitting there surrounded by such a beautiful circle of love – and she knew how to receive it – and being a contributing part of it.

Anne's story is rare, though. I've known so many more people whose Social Life diminishes with each day until they sit alone in front of a TV, waiting to die. Cultivating a healthy Social Life takes work. I get how it's something that suffers in today's modern society. But since I want to be like Anne, I need to make sure I keep looking at my daisy and reminding myself how important each petal is – especially that one since it's already droopy.

How is the health of your Social Life? Is it getting healthier or is your petal drooping too? And does it revolve around vices . . . or vegetables? Pick the veg!

Pixie's Rx

"I Belong to the Math Club, and the Science Club..." – One of my all-time favorite movies is "The Breakfast Club". I think I can recite 80% of it verbatim. I was a teen when it came out and it brought me a strange kind of relief that there would be a social world for me, too, if I could just find it. In my adult years I have found one of the best ways to meet new friends and expand my social circle is to join a free club, organization, or activity. Check your community for choirs, book clubs, gardening clubs, etc. Whatever your interests, see if there is a free club to enjoy. You never know what fun awaits!

Give It Some Time – I know none of the people I know – myself included – feel we have enough time. I get stingy with my time often, feeling that if I don't I'll end up without any time left to myself. My truth is, however, that I waste a whole bunch of "my time" every day. I find I do better when I have things in my schedule that take me out of the house – so I organize myself better around those pockets. Also, I have found that one of the best, most rewarding choices I can make with my time is to volunteer somewhere. Many organizations desperately need our help. Find a cause you can stand behind and give your time. I've met some of my favorite people volunteering. And I feel awesome hanging out with other volunteers. Those are some of the best parties ever!

Invent A New World – Years ago I met a neighbor who is quite introverted – even more so than I. In her shyness she often doesn't have extended conversations with you until she knows you better. From the outset, though, I really loved the energy she had, and I wanted to know her better. She had a dog. We have two. That helped us to say longer and longer hellos, but it wasn't until "The Doggie Intelligence Agency" (DIA) was formed that we really came to know one another better. The DIA consisted originally of her one dog and our two, and a series of "paw-written" notes between "the Agents" (our dogs and ourselves). Each of us has a code name and a distinct personality within the organization. As we told other friends of the DIA, they were intrigued. Since that time The Agency has grown and now contains over twenty Agents on three continents. Through our "Special Ops" we share in each other's worlds – and get to share pictures of our dogs too!

Through the Kindness of Strangers – I found myself in my mid-thirties with crumbling relationships everywhere, and a totally decimated social life. When I honestly looked at 'why?', I could see how I had cultivated a fairly repugnant Social persona for myself. I was SUCH a victim in every conversation. No wonder people were fleeing my side! So I started to work on being the world's most upbeat conversant whenever I met new people who hadn't already met Victim Girl. I couldn't be that upbeat Pixie with those I knew yet because it wasn't yet "me"! But stranger after stranger helped to cultivate the Me I Like To Be – and I get invited to parties again!

"I've Got A Barn" – Some of the most significant Social experiences in my life have come from theatre. There is something so magical about being a part of a theatre production. Those involved often become a family and tight, open, resilient relationships emerge. Get thee to a community theatre nearby – immediately! If performing isn't your thing, even better! Community theatres need all sorts of support, from box office staff (a really fun job!), to ushers, to set builders, to costumers, to spotlight operators! There are many capacities to fill. If your Social Life is struggling, community theatre is a great tool! Try it.

Here's To the Ladies Who Lunch – For a time I was part of a Ladies Lunch Quartet. It was awesome. Each month we picked a date and place, and met for a long lunch in order to chat and stay connected. We often included others as well, but the Core Four is what I remember the most. My father had a Men's Luncheon he attended every week with various men from his community. One of his brothers was often in attendance, and when my husband came to town he was invited to join. I saw how that weekly meal lit my father up, which was vitally important since he had a very tough cancer for the last few years of his life. Even on days that he felt horrible, my father attended lunch. And, it always helped him to feel better. Find a few people interested in a Brown Bag Brigade. Meet once a month, share stories, and enjoy connecting with one another.

Prairie Play – Before we had a world of machinery to "do" for us, we used our hands to make things. Each time I watch "Little House on the Prairie" I'm reminded of how much they used their hands – and they were often together and sharing stories while doing so. Quilting bees, backing days, canning, harvest time, etc. Even in my own childhood there were days filled with hand cranking tomato juice into glass canning jars. There needed to be at least three of us to efficiently do the work, and consequently conversation ensued. Why not seek out a modern day bee? Or contact one of your local organic farms and ask if you can help them can in the fall. Not only will your social calendar benefit, but you'll get to learn "new" stuff too!

A Family That Plays Together . . . – Call one of your family members. One you haven't spoken to for ages. See what they're up to. How are they doing? See who they are now. Families used to be tightly knit cohesive units out of necessity. As such, they fulfilled a huge Social function, as well. In our modern world, staying connected to family is mostly a choice, and one often not taken. Whatever the reasons, look for a family member to reconnect with. I've recently re-found my first-cousin-once-removed, Jane. We have had a blast attending free concerts in the part, game nights at our Castle, and contra-dancing in the Village. We compare family notes and give our opinions of particular events. Not only do I get a "date", but it ends up being informatively therapeutic, too.

Become Barbara Walters – "People love to talk about themselves." A truer phrase was never uttered. I remember the first time I grasped that concept. I was backstage at "Mary Poppins" on Broadway. One of our young stagehands was lamenting that he felt awkward at parties – never knowing what to say – and so he didn't attend. A lovely person, Jane Carr, liltingly stated, "Oh darling, it's EASY! Just ask people questions – where you from, what you do, etc. – and that's it. People LOVE to talk about themselves. Just ask a few questions and you'll never have to worry again." So, I tried her idea. And it was AWESOME! Not only did it make meeting people a breeze, and once you ask someone about her/himself, they like *you* much more! Plus, it gives me the opportunity to really see people and decide who I might want to share my story with – or not. Interview others; after all, you are seeing if you'd like to accept them into your future stories!

I Believe . . . – What does your heart believe? For some people the answer is in education, while others go toward spiritual pursuits. Still others may prefer escapism or creative pursuits. Whatever your heart believes is DIVINE can lead you to others who feel the same. Speak from your heart to others who can hear and embody your words. Being amongst FELLOW BELIEVERS is a relief of grand proportion to the soul. Ever see an "outcast" find "their kind"? Suddenly a lone soul became part of a community and healing and joy can immediately be felt. Search your heart for what it believes. Then hang with your homeys . . . because you will FINALLY feel HOME.

Pixie's Yumspiration
Tremendous Tacos

Suggested Ingredients: Onion, Garlic, Portobello Mushrooms, Black Beans (pre-cooked), Olive Oil, Tomato, Zucchini, Cilantro, Salt, Pepper, Cumin, Chili Powder, Paprika, Taco Shells, Cheddar Cheese, Jalapeno Peppers, Sour Cream, Taco Sauce

Preparation: Chop all veg. In a skillet, sauté all but mushrooms in olive oil until just softened. Add mushrooms and black beans. Mix thoroughly. Add all spices. Mix, cover, and simmer for a few minutes while taco shells are warming in the oven (according to directions on package). Serve with cheese, jalapeno peppers, sour cream and taco sauce.

Consumer Quote: (from a 16-year old girl) "There won't be any leftovers of these tonight!" (There weren't.)

Chapter 14

-Spirituality-

Finding My Light

I've set and achieved many, many goals so far in my lifetime. I don't see that changing very soon. I get a kick out of all the steps I need to take to manifest something I've dreamt I wanted. I'm also equally delighted when serendipity comes a callin' and vision becomes a plan, becomes a reality – and very, very quickly. Either way (or any way in between) I love reaching a goal.

As the years went on, however, my goals seemed to keep getting less and less ambitious – except when it came to my health. My goal there has been – and continues to be – of a very high standard for myself. And, for me, it turns out that embracing "HEALTH" as a virtue has brought with it all sorts of beneficial friends and relatives along with it. I've been able to see how "Being Healthy" needs to have a constant, active component to it or it will deteriorate quickly and go away.

The final piece of my puzzle was learning to listen to my Spirit. What was that sweet inner voice saying to me? "Go to the light, Kate. Not death, but the light of a vibrant, bright life." My Spirit was asking me – is STILL asking me – "How has your life become so dim?" At the worst of it I only had a couple of hours of "light" each week. I felt horrible on every level. At the best of it – which is today, – always "today" – I keep Regard My Spirit on my daily TO DO checklist. Everyday I strive to be as vibrant, healthy, joyful, and full of light as I can. I also strive to learn how to cultivate more of that awesomeness in my life going forward.

Sometimes I can't turn the dimmer switch up on all areas of my life at once. Sometimes an area is so undeveloped that it needs my concentrated energy and the other aspects of myself that remain well lit on the whole function without much effort for short periods of disregarded time.

Spirituality has been my area of darkness since I was a very, very young girl. I remember starting out this life as a vibrantly Spiritual being. I had conversations and playtime with my "angels and fairies everywhere". I saw them in the trees and in the water and in a sparkly diamond. We hung out and they comforted me during painful times at home, and, later, when all the sickness began. My angels and fairies calmed me, made me laugh inside, and allowed me escape from the heaviness of growing up in a household defined by sickness and the impending loss of a parent.

Early on, however, I spoke of them in my childhood church. To my utter anguish the Sunday School teacher immediately informed me that there are not fairies, and that while angels DO exist, we cannot talk to them or see them until we die. And then she told me I should pray and ask Jesus' forgiveness for believing in false gods. Essentially she said my precious, healing angels and fairies were the work of SATAN trying to lure me into his trap.

I was crushed. And scared. I didn't want to be lured into Satan's plan and condemned to an eternity of hellfire and damnation. I wanted to do what was "right", "correct", and as close to perfection as humanly possible (although I was assured I would never achieve perfection while still here on Earth). Perfection was a human impossibility and I was sinful and arrogant to think that I could be perfect in any way.

Except, the words I learned from various teachers within my childhood religion didn't always ring true for me. I had glimmers of knowing that "they" – the believers of such a narrow scope of life paths – were simply uninformed. Not even *mis*informed, but rather, they didn't know out of ignorance. That's all. And I also know, somewhere, that there were some people for whom ignorance really IS bliss, and that's ok.

I remember my fairies transporting me away to magic lands when I was having frequent colonoscopies as a child. Between the harshness of the prep and being fully conscious for the exams, I needed to find some place of solace and retreat. My precious, beautiful fairies led me to such a place. They taught me to trust their lead through gentle kindness and they came through for me each and every time.

Just recently I put all their gifts together in a pile and really examined the bounty I received. Firstly, when I began to take singing lessons, my teachers never really taught me the "correct way" to breathe. There would be slight tweaks to my breathing for phrasing purposes, but nobody ever taught me how to engage the diaphragm to support my tone. They didn't need to. The fairies had already taught me how.

When I was having my colon exams, the fairies taught me how to engage my diaphragm, allow it to lead my breath, and ostensibly be my inner anesthesia. Breathing fully into the body this way allows for the central nervous system to be calmed and soothed, thereby relaxed me and gave me the ability to withstand really long, painful, embarrassing procedures.

By the time I started singing in earnest at the age of twelve, I had already had two years of Fairy Breathing Technique Classes, and far too many forced opportunities to practice it. So by the time I began study with my first teacher at age fifteen, I was quite a proficient Fairy Breather. That proficiency allowed me to get really good, really fast, as a singer. And I loved every single second of it. It was healing making those noises, making music, breathing in so deeply, and relaxing the body and communing with the angels – *my* angels.

And that's about the point my Spiritual self went to sleep for about thirty years. Oh Spiritual Me would occasionally turn over and snort something or engage in a vivid dream, but mostly she slept, rested her weary, battered, confused self, and allowed the healing power of sleep to prevail. My angels and fairies had taken me as far as they could at that point, given the weekly teachings that so vehemently counseled against such "insanity and sin".

After giving me the tool of singing to keep me alive, I was left to find my own path, mostly in the dark – except when I would lose myself in the soothing escape of singing. And without the angels' and fairies' companionship when I was alone, I began to attach external characters to my song, thus beginning an internal war between my EGO and my FAITH. Faith that I only could attain glimmers of while bathed in the vibration of my own voice attached to a melody. But then my EGO immediately stepped in and took all the credit once it was up for grabs.

Over the years I lost the humbleness it is necessary to live inside of in order to truly love that connection with the Divine. My voice became trapped inside my body; defined by the Rules of this Earth. I began to abhor the very sound of it. I began to resent that it existed, that I had followed it to the jungle of New York City, and that I had allowed the seductive promise of fame and fortune to rob me of all security and hope for an easy future.

And then I stopped singing altogether. Unless I "had to" due to a paycheck I felt was large enough to withstand the pain, or if the gig was high profile enough. Who could I meet there? Would it be worth the time and pain of having to listen to "IT", "HER", that strident screecher I carried inside my throat. I read Nora Ephron's book "I Feel Bad About My Neck." I wanted to add a chapter about becoming disenchanted with the mechanism within.

I began to hear shades of my mother's voice creeping into my own. I felt "My Voice" had left me. I irrationally feared I would soon transition into a long, slow decline of watching my vibrato become semi-truck wide and difficult to enjoy by either the listener or me as I was producing it. All of these things compounded to eventually paralyze me into one bad performance after another. Each gig I got I forgot my lyrics, couldn't remember the melody all of the sudden, or I produced tones that were outside "my pocket" and so therefore sounded strained, unpleasant, and unlike me.

For years I had heard women friends of mine say how when they reached their forties they became plagued with stage fright. Suddenly they were unable to perform to their previous levels, almost – it seemed – overnight. Much like athletes who have to move on, I saw that very few actresses go the distance of time. Most leave the profession in their late thirties or early forties, leaving a few incredible divas behind to carry on for all us that had that childhood dream.

But I never thought it would happen to me.

And then it did.

I remember the exact moment it came to visit me. I was asked to sing at my closest girlfriend's wedding. She had written a song and arranged it for two soloists – a man and a woman – and eight or so ensemble voices. She wrote the song with my voice in mind. And it was *beautiful*. At the time she sent it to me to learn, I was on tour with "Mary Poppins". One day, not long before the wedding, I opened the electronic file and set to work on it inside my hotel room before my evening performance.

As I sat there working on the song, I started thinking of all the famous people who might be in attendance. My friend is quite well connected and I became obsessed with the sheer number of "important people" who would be there and able to hear me. I wasn't in the back, blending into the ensemble (which contained at least one Tony-nominated person). No, she put *me* center stage at the most important moment of her life that far to sing her song.

And I froze. I messed it up. In my preparation I trapped myself inside of my ego and I had zero faith that my loving friend wouldn't have asked me to do anything that would embarrass me. No, this was the culmination of the war that had been raging for years between my ego and my Spirit. And my oh-so-ignored Spirit lost the battle fully and completely – again. It was utterly decimated in the fight and it lay under my vengeful ego's feet, so small and sad.

So, I stopped "singing". My ego led my body to whatever gig my Spirit could stomach, although those were getting fewer and fewer to find. I started saying no to almost everything, and those things I did initially commit to were either cancelled at the last minute, or half-assed and resented at the execution thereof.

But then, after my Spirit rested for a while, it started giving me gifts again to see if I was ready to stop wearing myself out with ego yet. One of the most profound of these gifts was the return of an old friend into my life. And she brought with her my voice. It turns out I had left the love of it in her care and now she was returning it to me.

In my mid-twenties, just after the loss of "Side Show" on Broadway had battered me, I was cast as Janis Joplin in a production of "Beehive". The music director was a fun-loving, spunky woman named Mary Ann. I fell in love with her immediately. She had swagger and confidence and she commanded her band and the stage with immense acuity. I set out to make my way into her inner sanctum and have her compose songs for me.

And I was successful. We became fast friends and she immediately fell in love with my voice and began hiring me for gigs. She also quickly started composing songs with my voice in her head. And they are glorious compositions. I remember one song she wrote for me sent me to the moon the first time I wrapped my voice around its melody. For about five years she frequently hired me to sing – and gave me kudos and accolades and kind guidance each time she did.

But then Broadway became my bread and butter. I no longer was available for most of her gigs, coupled with her work transferring out of town, and ultimately overseas for a time. Over the course of several years we had stopped collaboration as artists and as a result our friendship also waned. I simply became "too busy" and that fun spot in my musical and social life dimmed to almost nothing but an email or phone call here and there.

At my lowest point of despair – friendless, creatively blocked, lonely to the core – an email popped into my box, "I'm back!" I immediately replied and asked when we could hang out. A plan was made, a date set and – like old times – we were going to eat at my place and hang out at the piano all night. Even though I still wasn't singing I was immediately excited about the prospect of trying to do so with her.

Over the course of the next few months, Mary Ann and I got together frequently and hungrily we played and sang together for hours each week. She taught me to sing jazz – until then a scary land of "I CAN'T!!!" that had eluded me for years. We also told each other our stories from the years when we hadn't made time to share with each other.

It was during these months that my Spirit began to find Her beautiful strength and ability to expand. The healing power of music helped me to escape and have respite from the deep-rooted anxiety that has been with me for so long. And, the stories! Being able to tell my tales to an attentive and listening audience has allowed me to enjoy my journey and relish in its slowly unfolding beauty.

I still have a long way to grow. And I can't wait for each new bud to appear on my tree. For each new leaf, flower and expanded root system, that adds to the overall intrinsic beauty of my life, to be seen. I seek out light – knowing that I need it to grow, and to clearly see the places that have already begun to do so.

When on stage I am always conscious of "finding my light." I love the stage. I love to be on it. And, I love to be in the spotlight while up there. There are few better feelings in this world than stepping into My Light and feeling it bathe over me. Before my life on stage I didn't understand the concept of seeking out my own light. I had been taught that my light was to come from within – and while that is ultimately true, I believe – but not understanding the concept, I simply stayed lost in the dark. Once I was fortunate enough to find my escape on the boards, a very valuable truth became known to me: Whether it comes from within or without – find your light. And bathe in it for growth.

And now, the wisdom of The Arts has helped me grow in my life once again. Each day I look to find my light; that part of me that is capable of being the "me" I feel I was before life and religion confused my Spirit and scared her into her slumber.

In church one of my favorite songs was "This Little Light of Mine". The lyrics are:

> This little light of mine.
> I'm gonna let it shine.
> This little light of mine.
> I'm gonna let it shine,
> Let it shine,
> Let it shine,
> Let it shine.

I felt good singing that song. It was one of the first ones I ever learned and while "Satan" and "Jesus" are leading characters of later verses, I didn't yet know who they were when I first learned that song. They were barely yet introduced to me and I still had my unadulterated natural inclination to listen to my angels' and fairies' voices with utter joy and abandonment on a daily basis. While their "removal" from my story might have stunted my Spirit for a time, I am happy to say that today She is full of light, love, strength, and optimism for each and every moment we will share together on this Earth, inhabiting this Body, and utilizing this Mind to constantly help me to learn more, be more, and love more.

Oh, and I eat tons and tons of vegetables.

Pixie's Rx

Meditation – Just Google it and you'll find dozens and dozens of FREE resources introducing and teaching the practice of meditation. There are many different forms, and all help to repair and grow one's Spiritual self. Also, in my experience, a little goes a long way, so no big time investment necessary. Just a few minutes a day is all it takes. This is a cumulative practice.

Yoga – Again, consult the Googler. Or go to the library to check out some books or DVDs. Also, various stores, community centers, churches, etc. offer free yoga classes, so check in your local area for possible freebies. You can do yoga anywhere, in any attire. In focusing your eye gaze and breath, the Mind, Body, and Spirit all have a chance to work in harmony, thus giving a pathway for Spiritual growth to occur. Also, it's fun. And it makes you feel great, and look vibrant and healthy, too.

Church – This one is obvious, and I KNOW the point is to pay into a church, but I feel that's only appropriate if you become a member of the congregation. I encourage everyone to go out and experience different faiths and how those faiths worship with each other. So many services are simply beautiful to attend, even if you don't believe the dogma of the particular sect. Also, it can often clear up any misunderstandings or false or ignorant teachings that may have taught you to fear another faith. At the core, each religion asks us the same things: LOVE. . . and "do unto others", in some form or another. I do feel, however, from my experience, this should be an adult-only sport. Religion is advanced stuff and many of its core subjects – sex, death, morality, for example – are simply inappropriate to discuss in depth with young minds. At a certain level, it's abusive. Since that was my childhood religious tale I ask that we all please be careful to treat religion as the powerful medicine that it is. It has the power to simultaneously unite and divide people – with extreme passion and often very little reason. This one's free….but don't let it cost you – or anyone else!

Ambulando, Baby – Go outside and walk! In all weather. This absolutely produces Spiritual growth cumulatively over time. Even five minutes can rejuvenate. Solvitur Ambulando! It IS solved by walking!

Define Your Divine In Your Mind – Different from meditation, but often lumped together with it, prayer is an awesome Spiritual tool. It can truly help you to better define and align your own personal beliefs. When you pray, whom are you talking to? What is their name or moniker? Do they have a gender? Since a deity is a very private, inner relationship and cannot be harnessed or seen outwardly by others, you can have a ball with this one. Open your heart, really talk to – and SEE YOUR DEITY when you pray. When I close my eyes and see mine, my Spirit soars and I don't feel so alone when I'm low.

Create Something – A plan, a dream, a piece of art, a conversation, a project, a sacred space, a "Nouveau Normale"….. anything, but put your mind to the task of creating something to feed your Spirit….which, in turn, helps keep your Spiritual practices vibrant and clicking. Your Spirit wants to participate in life and creating is one of its favorite Invitations to Participation.

Mirror, Mirror, On the Wall – "Who is the reflection? And how is she (he) called?" I forgot to look in the mirror for about ten years. When I started again, that question popped into my head every time I saw my own reflection. Look into your own eyes and ask yourself kind, insightful questions. Then, depart your own gaze with a simple, "I love you, (insert own name here)". Say it even if you don't mean it. Even if it doesn't ring true today. It will in time, with practice. Loving yourself is one of the greatest Spiritual practices of all times.

Where Does Dewey Decimal Keep the Self-Help Books?
– Go to your public library and lose yourself in the stacks. Explore what others have written about Spirituality and what exploring it did for them. Where did they find their path? Plus, there's nothing more healing on a cold, rainy day than tucking into the soothing quiet and musty smells of a local library. It is a sanctuary of learning where you can set your Spirit to run free.... for free.

Compose Some Prose – Write a poem and compose a melody to send your words toward the heavens. Take your time. Don't rush. Write to your deity about it. Make your own musical conversations occur. It doesn't have to be long, but it can be, if you want. This is a private creation just for you. Just let your heart speak...and watch your Spirit soar through your piece.

Small, Gentle Change – Choose one of the suggested practices and devote ten minutes per week to its completion. Note in a journal what you did, how you rate it, did it have an impact, etc. Keep working at that change if you enjoy it, or move to another one and repeat the process. When you feel ready and able, add another free practice with another ten-minute block per week, for a total of twenty minutes per week devoted to growing your Spirituality. Work up to twenty to thirty minutes per day – or to whatever level feels perfect for you. Adjust levels as needed throughout your life. Enjoy!

Pixie's Yumspiration
Rhubarb Compote

Suggested Ingredients: Rhubarb, Cinnamon, Nutmeg, Fresh Ginger Root, Orange Extract, Maple Syrup, Water

Preparation: Finely chop rhubarb and ginger root. Put pieces into a saucepan and cover with water (plus ½ inch). Add ginger root. Bring to a boil. Once at boil, stir, cover, reduce heat, and allow mixture to simmer until rhubarb is softened. Once that occurs, add orange extract and a dash of maple syrup. Stir, and continue to simmer until rhubarb disintegrates. Serve warm or cold over yogurt, ice cream, or cake.

Consumer Quote: (from an 41-year old man) "Rhubarb is scary, but if I don't think about it, this is good."

Epilogue

This summer I planned a solitary existence for myself so that I could edit and publish this book on time. Shortly into my semi-solitary confinement in Vermont my father became terribly, horribly ill and I was needed in Ohio to support him and my mother during the end of his life.

As I left my idyllic Vermont sanctuary, I wondered if I could maintain any of the advice I've given in this book during what was sure to be a trying time. My father was in ICU. I knew that meant we weren't going home with him any time soon – if at all. I left the serenity of Vermont and was thrust into the chaos of The Cleveland Clinic, where my father lay clinging to his life. I went from the vibrancy and life of nature in Vermont to the coldness and death of a giant behemoth of a hospital, in a formerly industrial city. Given this extreme swing, how would I do?

All in all, I would have to give myself a B-plus - and I'm happy with that. I spent two months total caring for my parents while my father passed on. I stayed on couches, in hotels, at a friend's home, at my friend's mother-in-law's home, on the floor beside my father's bed, and finally, I slept in my childhood bedroom – the same place where all my sickness began to take root all those years ago. Many nights I "tried" to sleep. Many nights I settled for a state of meditation. Other nights I magically got enough deep sleep to carry me through the next day's enormous tasks. I was tethered to my father's bedside, waiting for the doctors to come by with news of the next step. I ate whenever I could, whatever I could, and much of the time had no access to a kitchen of my own. My daily walking regime went from an average of five miles a day to an average of one mile a day. I was away from everyone and everything I am used to having around me. And, in spite of those obstacles, I still managed not to revert to becoming sick myself, as I used to do so often.

Was I perfect? No. Not at all. I give myself B-plus. I passed enough of the "tests" and turned in enough of the "assignments" that I was able to come out "passing the course" – and learning an immense amount about it, too. I learned where the Modern Medical System is today and what it offers to its patients while inside of its care. I learned how to get the best out of people – including myself – and to learn to love life better in the process. I learned that all my Pixie's Prescriptions are as good today as they were when I first employed them for myself, and each subsequent time afterward. And I learned that even as one is dying, much of the medicine I've written about in here is still vitally healing – no matter what stage of life one is in.

My father passed away at home, surrounded by his loved ones. He lived heartily inside that home, despite some really debilitating – irreversible – issues. Many of the prescriptions in this book came from his example. He received a "death sentence" at the age of thirty, yet lived vibrantly until age seventy-three. Nothing will make us live forever, but many things can help us live A Feel Better Life. So, I'll keep looking at my beautiful, sparkly daisy, and live its parts each day, as best I can. And a B-plus grade is fine by me.

Acknowledgements

I've been trying to write a book now for several years. My first attempt was a long, rambling mess of a thing that was more exploration into my head than a viable book. Along this journey I've had wonderful friends who read my work, lovingly critiqued it, and helped me to grow – and finally achieve my goal.

At the top of the list of supporters, by far, is my mother, Linda Coffman. My mother has supported me in every way possible, above and beyond what I've seen other parents do for their kids. She's just incredible in her immense capacity to encourage me to keep taking the next step – especially when I'm ready to abandon ship.

A special thanks also goes to Joshua Rosenthal of the Institute for Integrative Nutrition for his teaching and encouragement. It is due to his pairing with the lovely Lindsey Smith and creating a place of guidance for first-time authors that this book was finally completed and published. Thank you Joshua and Lindsey for your passion, your enthusiasm, your support, and your desire to give of your knowledge to others.

Thank you to my awesome friends – especially Andrea Natalie, David White, Rob Jackson, Eileen Tepper, Tachi Taylor, Paul Maggio, Paul Zablocki, Randy Losapio, Anne and Bob Persico, Cousin Jane Williams, Sue Elias, Teri Hirss, Seth Rudetsky, Cedric Thompson, and Kareena Denman – for support, encouragement, and many laughs along the way. Thank you to my clients for sharing their journeys with me, and for teaching me as I coach them. I also thank the amazing Oprah Winfrey for providing such a great introduction to some of today's most incredible thinkers. Her programs have helped to educate me in immensely valuable ways. I don't know her – yet – but I appreciate what a great teacher she has been to me. Thank you, Ms. Winfrey.

Most importantly. thank you to my family. You have lived through much of my healing, and have lovingly journeyed with me through it. To Johnny and Eddie, for inspiring me to keep getting better. Thank you, Mer, for your warmth, your love, your support, your inspiration, and your humor. You are my greatest teacher, my PIC, my SW. I thank you for being you. And, the biggest "Thank you" of all goes to my husband, Ed Chapman. You saw me when I didn't yet see me. And you stayed with me through the gnarly parts. I love you – and I love our family.

I hope this book is fun and helpful for all who choose to open its pages. May we all find fun, free things to use as medicine when that's what's appropriate. And, most of all, may we all have A Feel Better Life. Now go eat some veg!